THE LAUGHING BUDDHA:
Zen and the Comic Spirit

THE LAUGHING BUDDHA:

Zen and the Comic Spirit

Self-portrait in the image of Pu-tai HAKUIN

THE LAUGHING BUDDHA
Zen and the Comic Spirit

by Conrad Hyers

Wipf & Stock
PUBLISHERS
Eugene, Oregon

Wipf and Stock Publishers
199 West 8th Avenue, Suite 3
Eugene, Oregon 97401

The Laughing Buddha
Zen and the Comic Spirit
By Hyers, Conrad
Copyright©1989 by Hyers, Conrad
ISBN: 1-59244-495-4
Publication date 1/26/2004
Previously published by Longwood Academic, 1989

In Gratitude to

Masao Abe, Eliot Deutsch, and Derek Southall
For their help and encouragement

Contents

Illustrations

8

Acknowledgments

I should like to express my appreciation for a Ford Foundation Asian Studies Grant, enabling me to participate in a faculty conference on Buddhism at Carleton College, where the fledgling outlines of this book were hesitantly advanced, and where I profited from the reservations, doubts, and encouragements of the colleagues of that experience, especially Joseph Kitagawa, Winston King, Bardwell Smith, Walpole Rahula, David Yu, Frank Reynolds, and Frank Wong. Appreciation is also due for another Non-Western Studies Fellowship from the Ford Foundation which supported a term of research and writing at the University of Hawaii and the East-West Center; for a Younger Humanist Fellowship from the National Endowment for the Humanities which provided sabbatical time for further development of the manuscript; and for a fellowship from the Fund for the Study of the Great Religions which afforded a leave from teaching responsibilities for study and dialogue in Japan.

Special acknowledgment must be given to Eliot Deutsch, in whom the preliminary essay of the project struck a responsive chord, and to *Philosophy East and West*, of which he was the editor, for publishing it under the title, "The Ancient Zen Master as Clown-Figure and Comic Midwife." Similar acknowledgment is due Masao Abe, and the editorial board of *The Eastern Buddhist* of which he is a member, for encouraging the publication of the materials of Chapter Five in an issue of that journal under the title, "The Comic Perspective in Zen Literature and Art." Derek Southall, editor of *The Middle Way*, likewise gave his encouragement by offering portions of Chapter Six in that periodical under the titles "Zen and the Commonplace" and "Zen and the Comic Acceptance of the Absurd,"

I am also indebted to Christmas Humphreys of the London Buddhist Society, Ben Kimpel of Drew University, Thomas Berry of Fordham University, and Joseph Campbell of Sarah Lawrence College, whose kind letters of enthusiasm and suggestion provided welcome inspiration at critical junctures of the writing. Gratitude must go, too, to the various Zen masters and Buddhist scholars who gave me the benefit of their reactions and criticisms during my visits to Japan, particularly Nanrei Kobori, Sohaku Ogata, Eshin Nishimura, Shojun Bando, and Masao Abe. A very special appreciation is to be given to the Soto monks of Soji-ji monastery who permitted the opportunity of sharing in their common life. I should also like to give due recognition to my children, Jon, Dean, and Lauri, whose innocent playfulness and laughter have frequently interrupted these labors with a nostalgic reminder of the "little Zen" of the child, and a foretaste of the "foolishness" of the sage. It is, in part, in relation to those childlike experiences of wonder and acceptance, of carefree immediacy and spontaneous delight, that these essays stand as a kind of remembrance, a recollection and a return on a higher level no doubt, but to those truths which are always and everywhere known, yet so easily forgotten.

> *Your singing and dancing is none other than*
> *the voice of Dharma.*
>
> *Zazen Wasan,* Hakuin

The author wishes to thank the publishers who have given permission to use material from their publications as indicated in the 'Notes' to chapters and also to the following:

Edmund R. Brill, *The Basic Writings of Sigmund Freud,* translated and edited by A.A. Brill, © 1938 by Random House Inc.; renewed © 1965 by Gioia B. Berheim and Edmund R. Brill. Reprinted by permission.
Doubleday and Company Inc.: *An Introduction to Haiku* by Harold G. Henderson, © 1958. Reprinted by permission.
  Zen: Poems, Prayers, Sermons, Anecdotes, Interviews by Lucien Stryk and Takashi Ikemoto, © 1963, 1965. Reprinted by permission.
Faber and Faber Ltd: *Sengai, The Zen Master* by D.T. Suzuki, © 1971 by the Matsugaoka Bunko Foundation. Plates 34 and 40 and quotations used by permission of Faber and Faber Ltd and the Matsugaoka Bunko Foundation.
  A History of Zen Buddhism by Heinrich Dumoulin, S.J., translated by Paul Peacey, © 1963. Reprinted by permission of Faber and Faber Ltd, all rights reserved.

11

Charles E. Tuttle Inc.: *The Iron Flute* by N. Senzaki and Ruth McCandless, © 1961.

Zen and Oriental Art by Hugo Munsterberg, © 1965. Plates 4, 5 and 24 and quotations reprinted by permission.

Zen Flesh, Zen Bones by Paul Reps and Nyogen Senzaki, © 1957.

Viking Press Inc.: *The Masks of God: Primitive Mythology* by Joseph Campbell, © 1969. Reprinted by permission.

Acknowledgment is also gratefully given to the following for permission to use reproductions of original paintings and sketches:

Benrido Company, Kyoto, for a scene from *Choju-Giga*.

Boston Museum of Fine Arts, for "Three Sages Laughing on Tiger Creek," Japanese, Post Ashikaga, ink monochrome by Soga Shohaku (right fold of a two-fold screen), Bigelow Collection.

Eisei Bunko Foundation, Tokyo, for "Tan-hsia Burning the Buddha Image" and "The Meditating Frog" by Sengai, from the Sazo Idemitsu Collection.

Freer Art Gallery, Washington, D.C., for the cover art: "Crazy Monk" (Gama Sennin) by Soga Shohaku.

Kosetsu Museum of Art, Kobe, for the "Dancing Pu-tai" by Liang-k'ai from the Murayama Collection.

Mr. Takanaru Mitsui for "Hui-neng Tearing Up the Sutras" by Liang-k'ai, from his private collection.

Shokokuji, Kyoto, for the "Tenth Cow-herding Picture" by Shubun.

Tokyo National Museum for "Han-shan and Shih-te" by Yen-hui.

I regret that I have been unable to locate the present owner of "Bodhidharma" by Matabei, originally housed in the T. Takeoka Collection.

12

CHAPTER ONE

The Other Side of Zen

A million Mount Sumerus are but a drop of dew
On the end of a single hair;
Three thousand worlds are only a seagull
Floating on the ocean waves.
The two children of the tiny creatures
In the eyebrow of a mosquito
Never stop quarrelling between themselves
As to whose earth this is.

HAKUIN[1]

In writing a book about Zen one has the double sensation of attempting, on the one hand, to compress a million Mount Sumerus into the tip of a single hair, and, on the other hand, to inflate the utter simplicity of a single hair into a million Mount Sumerus. One also has the haunting suspicion that one is turning into an argument, a debate, perhaps even a quarrel, what is only available as a fundamental intuition and experience which no amount of discussion in itself can effect, and which may simply result in a dispute as to who possesses authentic title to what is freely open to all.

On how to sing
The frog school and the skylark school
Are arguing.

Shiki[2]†

The radically intuitive, experiential and wordless character of Zen does not easily lend itself to book form, as anyone who has entertained the notion of writing about Zen, or the prospect of being taken for an authority on the subject, is inevitably aware. There is a certain humor in the very suggestion of offering a book on Zen, let alone on Zen and humor, which is not unlike propositioning a man with

---

† *Dates of Zen masters, poets, and artists cited are given in the Index. In the case of most Chinese names, Japanese pronunciations are also given.*

a fish and giving him a stone—or an embalmed cat! Any addition, accordingly, to the already long parade of books which Zen has elicited in recent decades—no matter how neglected and important its theme, or how unique and intriguing its approach—must be willing to be placed, from the start, within the comic parenthesis of Master Chaochou's exclamation on joining the funeral procession for one of his monks: "What a long train of dead bodies follows in the wake of a single living person!"[3]

Yet hopefully, despite these and other limitations, the reception will be more favorable than that which Bodhidharma, the first patriarch of Chinese Zen (Ch'an), is alleged to have given to one of the Chinese classics when brought before him in order to solicit his reaction to its significance. Taking the book, he put it to his nose: "It has a kind of quarrelsome smell about it!"[4]

The Oddity of Zen

There are many ways into the way of Zen. Essays and books have been written on Zen in its relationship to art, archery, the tea ceremony, the martial arts, haiku poetry, the Noh theater, gardening, flower arrangement, and even cookery. But of these various ways, or even of the ways added by foreign and largely alien interests in psychoanalysis, comparative philosophy, and theology, to approach Zen from the standpoint of its relationship to the comic spirit will no doubt appear to be, at first sight, the oddest and most oblique—as well as the most likely to stir a controversy between the skylark school and the frog school!

On the one hand this reaction is entirely fitting, considering the place of the odd, the eccentric, and the outlandish in humor, clowning, and comedy as part of their very point and play. This *is* the odd way into Zen. But it is also the odd way of Zen itself, and an important part of the oft-noted oddity of Zen. It is, therefore, not nearly so odd in relation to Zen as it might appear to be in relation to any other religious tradition, whether within or without the Buddhist world. Where else could one meet a stranger assortment of spiritual guides, teaching methods, and religious expressions? In no other tradition could the entire syndrome of laughter, humor, comedy, and "clowning" be said to be more visible and pronounced than in Zen,

14

where the comic spirit has been duly rescued from those miscellaneous and peripheral moments to which it is so commonly assigned and restricted. So much is this so that it is difficult to imagine authentic Zen, or to survey the unusual history of Zen, completely apart from the comic vision.

As remarkable and unique as this is, however, it is the one dimension of Zen that has been given the least attention and interpretation. To be sure, references to the prominence and importance of comic elements in Zen and Zen art are scattered through much of the literature on Zen; and two brief essays have been devoted to it in English by R.H. Blyth and D.T. Suzuki.[5] The significance of this, nonetheless, far exceeds the meager attention it has received. In no other religious movement are its principal records (comprised largely of anecdotes relating to the lives and sayings of masters), its techniques for spiritual realization, its art and aesthetic, and its portrayals of the spirit and style of those masters whom one is called to emulate, so intimately intertwined with the comic spirit and perspective.

It is not easy to identify the reasons for the neglect of this "other side" of Zen, except to attribute it to the widespread taboo against associating the comic too closely with the sacred. Comic elements of whatever sort, found in connection with religious forms, we are often inclined, at best, to relegate to some presumably minor and inferior category—something on the order of an embellishment, like spice added to rice, which may give a certain palatability to religion at the elementary level, or a reprieve from its rigors, but is not an essential ingredient, and decidedly not the stuff of the religious life itself. At worst, we are inclined to see the comic as a distraction from, if not an eventual negation of, the seriousness and earnestness and holiness of the religious task—to be moving away from rather than toward religious goals and spiritual attainments. As a result, in most traditions outside of Zen, the various protagonists of the comic —whether iconoclast, humorist, clown or fool—have been barred from the temple precincts, and kept strolling in the streets, or imprisoned under ecclesiastical interdicts.

Such prejudices, often shared by priest and scholar alike, reflect a failure to understand the importance, in fact necessity, of the interplay between the sacred and the comic. Much too hastily it is presupposed that the comic is either so trivial that it has nothing to

15

say, or that it is so pointed in what it has to say that it is threatening and destructive. Yet the comic spirit and perspective plays a far greater and more significant role in religious experience and expression than priestly safe-keeping and scholarly investigation have been ready to admit or careful to recognize.

The Laughing Buddha

One of the early Buddhological debates, in fact, was over the question whether the Buddha ever laughed, and if so in what manner and with what meaning. This debate ranks somewhat above the debate in Western medieval scholasticism over how many angels could comfortably dance on the head of a pin—though the Buddhist debate seems characteristic of scholasticism wherever it is found. The issues, however, do have important consequences, so important that they affect the way in which the whole of Buddhism is perceived, practiced, and lived.[6]

There were those among the Buddhist scholastics who would probably have preferred to believe that the Buddha never laughed at all, especially after his enlightenment experience at Bodhgaya. The Buddha's wisdom and the Buddha's mission seemed to require the ultimate in gravity and solemnity. There could, of course, be no objection to the suggestion that the youthful Siddhartha Gautama had laughed during his self-indulgent period in his father's palace. Indeed, laughter might well be seen as a characteristic expression of the materialism and sensuality of his early years, prior to his discovery of the Middle Way and the Four Noble Truths. Laughter seems inextricably bound up with both the pleasures of palace life and the very sources of suffering later identified as ego, desire, attachment, ignorance, and bondage. Relative to the fundamental problem of suffering (*dukkha*), laughter seems to represent the hollow, super-ficial, and finally empty levity of momentary delight (*sukha*), foolishly evading or ignoring the deeper issues of life and death.

The identification of laughter and humor with sensuality and self-indulgence is very common. Western medieval physiology determined that the seat of laughter was the spleen.[7] This not very intellectually or spiritually promising location likely derived from the belief that each bodily organ had a function, and this was the function assigned to the spleen. Laughter seems to well up from some dark, abysmal region. It belongs not to matters of the heart or head, but to the stomach, intestines, sex organs, and bladder. Such abdominal associations seem further verified inasmuch as three of the most common topics of comic conversation are the earthen trinity of food, sex, and evacuation—justly earning the designation "low comedy."

Laughter is also commonly personified by dubious and ambiguous characters: clowns, fools, jesters, simpletons, comedians, and tricksters. And there are kinds of laughter and humor that indulge in the elevation of one person or group over another, as in the case of racist or sexist or ethnic jokes. Here ego and pride are fortified, injustices and cravings are legitimated, and people are separated and alienated from one another.

Given such earthy, zany, and divisive associations, it is not surprising that laughter and humor are commonly seen as inappropriate to holy places and serious disputations. It is also understandable that Buddhist scholastics might have preferred to disassociate the Buddha entirely from laughter in his post-enlightenment life and teaching. The difficulty is that some sutras seem to suggest, if not state outright, that on such and such an occasion the Buddha laughed.

Nowhere is the significance of this laughter more profoundly appreciated and frequently displayed than in the Zen tradition—even to the point of employing low comedy. Here the intention and result is quite the opposite. Laughter leads toward the debunking of pride and the deflating of ego. It mocks grasping and clinging, and cools desire. It cuts through ignorance and precipitates insight. It turns hierarchies upside down as a prelude to collapsing them, and overcomes dualities and conflicts by embracing and uniting opposites. The whole intellectual and valuational structure of the discriminating mind is challenged, with a result that is enlightening and liberating.

Early Buddhism, especially in its Mahayanist forms, recognized a variety of methods, called *upaya*, which are an accommodation to the condition and needs of the person, and to the context in which the teaching is delivered. So if one requires a justification for the presence of the comic in Zen, one may see it as a species of *upaya*, a device for bringing the Buddha-dharma into conscious awareness and existential realization. Laughter and humor may function both as a technique for precipitating spiritual understanding and as an

17

expression of new levels of insight and freedom.

Running Sideways

Important as calling attention to this may be, nevertheless to write a book about Zen and the comic spirit demands a measure of hesitancy because of the understandable frustration and dismay, if not justifiable holy indignation, of Zennists over Western books on Zen. For Western Zen and Western interpretations of Zen often reflect more talent in revealing the nature of Westernization than that of Zen. It is not that Westerners are singularly impervious to and incapable of Zen, but that the cultural and religious background of the West commonly moves in such different and even alien directions that so often Zen is appropriated for the wrong reasons, fostered by half-correct or simply incorrect expectations and interpretations. As Nyogen Senzaki protested with respect to the Americanization of Zen: "[It] is running sideways writing books, lecturing, referring to theology, psychology, and what not. Someone should stand up and smash the whole thing to pieces. . . ."[8] This kind of "smashing," however, is itself characteristic of the iconoclastic temper of Zen and is an important part of the comic method and vision of Zen.

The present effort is no doubt a form of "running sideways" in pointing toward and appreciating these dimensions of Zen. Yet, like the person who runs back and forth along the river bank calling attention to the fact that it is actually possible to cross over to the other shore, there may be some value, however limited and provisional, in moving sideways in order to move forward. Just as surely, though, the fool is one who confuses a great expenditure of energy in running back and forth with the accomplishment of actually getting somewhere. From the Zen standpoint such a person is like the small boy who shifts nervously from one foot to the other, while the real problem is that he needs to go and find a lavatory. One master, indeed, is reputed to have replied, in answer to a monk's inquiry as to the present abode of the Buddha: "The Buddha is in the outhouse!" Once we have realized the comedy of our situation we are already on our way to Zen, which is itself an illustration of one of the many affiliations between Zen and the comic spirit.

Still, there is a certain precariousness in writing about the comic

18

spirit, as well as the Zen spirit, in any context. For as with all things in the realm of the spirit, to talk too long, to examine too meticulously, to pile qualification upon qualification and add theory to theory, is to be in danger of upsetting the delicate balance of that life which one wishes to understand, or of destroying the fragile tissue into which one wishes to breathe new life. Here, too, "the letter kills, while the spirit gives life." The book, therefore, no doubt omits many of those niceties of academic notation and qualification which might enable the operation to be more successful at the expense of killing the patient. Even at that, so long a discourse no doubt comes under the interdict of the ninth-century master Ling-ch'ui who said that explanations of fundamental matters were "like drawing legs on a painted snake."[9]

The book is not, of course, nearly as short as might exemplify Zen, which might well be more accurately illustrated simply by offering a few humorous anecdotes, and concluding with an abrupt *Ho!* Yet, in a context which is not steeped in Buddhism or Oriental culture, this has never been sufficient, and opens itself to too many misuses and misinterpretations. There is therefore a place for restrained interpretation; while at the same time it must be undertaken only from within a keen awareness of the comic awkwardness about the very proposal to analyze both Zen and the comic spirit. For analysis has a way of failing to participate in the very spirit which it would analyze, and therefore not only involving itself in an ironic self-contradiction, but in a violation and negation of that to which it is attempting to do justice.

Recognizing the awkwardness of this dilemma, the effort has been made, as far as the stubborn woodenness of language and sterility of verbal interpretation will permit, not only to point to but enter the spirit of Zen, and the comic spirit of Zen. From an academic standpoint this is a spirit and a perspective that must be defined, and defined with all due philosophical and psychological precision. Yet from a Zen standpoint it must, above all, be experienced, while academic definitions have a special facility for standing squarely in the way of such experience and its understanding from within that experience. Such, in fact, is the concern of many a Zen anecdote. Master Chao-chou, for example, was once asked, "When the entire body decomposes, something spiritual seems to remain. What becomes of it?'' As the monk awaited a disquisition which would clarify the doctrine, Chao-chou replied, "The wind is blowing again this morning!"[10]

It must be emphasized, then, that though there are many ways into the way of Zen, along with which the present approach may be classified, in the final sense there are *no* ways. It is not simply a matter of proceeding down a certain established path, or discovering some magic key that might unlock Wu-men's celebrated "gateless gate" to Zen experience. All ways into Zen are limited by the peculiarity that they never arrive at their destination; they are like an endless guided tour around the outside walls of one monastery after another. The pointing finger, however straight and accurate, never quite reaches the moon!

Fixing and Not Fixing the Standards

A wide range of terms have been introduced in an effort to point in the direction of this "other side" of Zen—terms which are loosely related, and in some of their forms not necessarily related, or simply not related at all: smiling, laughing, joking, clowning, as well as nonsense, humor, comedy, absurdity, foolishness, and playfulness. Obviously the concern here is not with any kind of smiling, laughing, joking and clowning, or with any kind of context in which these expressions may occur. Laughter may be sadistic, demented, nervous, morbid, crude, teasing, taunting, cynical, bitter. Humor may be a way of evading truth and avoiding responsibility. Joking may be a convenient vehicle for ridiculing others in order to magnify one's own position and fortify one's own prejudices. Comedy may contain expressions of hostility and aggression, fear and anxiety, and so forth. Certainly, therefore, laughter, smiling, and joking are not necessarily reliable indices of the comic spirit, nor are all kinds of nonsense, absurdity, and playfulness necessarily informed by the comic perspective.

It is to be acknowledged, in fact, that in putting together such a broad spectrum of terms and phenomena, albeit related, and however qualified, the result may be seen as guilty of the exhaustively conglomerate definition which Corbyn Morris in his *Essay Towards Fixing the True Standards of Wit, Humour, Raillery, Satire, and*

20

Ridicule, (1744), saw as the principal success and failure of Dr. Barrow's "Sermon Against Foolish Talking and Jesting":

> There being perhaps no variety, in all the extent of these subjects, which he has not presented to view in (his) description. . .For instead of exhibiting the properties of wit in a clearer light, and confuting the false claims which are made to it, he has made it his whole business to perplex it the more by introducing, from all corners, a monstrous troop of new and unexpected pretenders!

Such terms, nevertheless, serve to point in the direction of that "other side" of existence, and of the human spirit, which is only too commonly seen as outside, if not inimical to, religious concerns and spiritual attainments. In relation to the ultra-seriousness and anxiety, and consequently the fanaticism and dogmatism, which frequently accompany the intensities of religious conviction and commitment, this definitely contains an element of truth. For what unites all these lighter manifestations of the spirit is a lightheartedness and playfulness which refuses to absolutize, or to take with an inflexible and unqualified seriousness, anything—especially one's self and one's situation. In its highest Zen form, it is the refusal, born of the freedom and perspective which in Buddhism is known as enlightenment, to be contained within and defined by the vicious circle of grasping and clinging, and that resists the temptation to enter the bondage of attachment to anything, however consequential or sacred. At this point the "other side" of the comic and "this side" of seriousness and sacrality become one in the freedom of him who has gone beyond holy and unholy, sense and nonsense, having and not-having, self and other.

In stating the matter in this way, it is clear that we have to do here with a very special kind of spirit and perspective, which it will be the task of the following essays to attempt to delineate. It is a spirit and perspective, an outlook upon life and a way of life, which involves a very special stance and set of attitudes in relation to existence. It is a way of perceiving reality and of experiencing reality, of being real, and not just any parlor witticism, clownish caper, or comedian's trick that commands our attention. It is a way and an experiencing, in fact, which cannot finally be delineated. As Master Tao-ch'in

21

responded to a monk asking about the message brought by
Bodhidharma from India to China: "I will explain it to you if you
wait until I am dead."[11]

The Dragon's Song

Monk: "What is Tao?"
Ts'ao-shan: "A dragon singing in the dry wood."
*Monk: "I wonder whether there is anyone who can hear
this?"*
*Ts'ao-shan: "There is no one in the entire world who
does not hear this."*
*Monk: "I do not know what kind of composition the
dragon's song is."*
*Ts'ao-shan: "I also do not know; but all who hear it
lose themselves.'*

The Transmission of the Lamp[12]

22

CHAPTER TWO

The Smile of Truth

When one has understanding, one should laugh;
One should not weep.

HSUEH-T'OU

The smile of Asian peoples has often been represented, usually in the caricatures of politically inspired cartooning and the stereotypes of popular Caucasian imagination, to which both the Chinese and Japanese have been subjected. That smile, insofar as it corresponds to reality at all, has a profound basis in the unusual stress in both Chinese and Japanese culture upon the human sphere and the natural graces, and indeed upon the most practical, earthen, everyday phenomena of life. It is a smile that is grounded in the peculiarly Oriental aversion to the more abstract flights and ethereal delights of Indian and Western peoples, and a preference for the concrete, this-worldly, ordinary-human, even trivial moments of day-to-day existence. In fact, if one may speak of a special, and seldom appreciated, contribution of Asian peoples to world civilization, it is to be found here: in this smile and what it symbolizes.

A smile, of course, can mean many things. Here it may be said to represent a special sensitivity to the comic-mundane, a tender affection for the commonplace things of life. Or—relative to the spiritual other-worldliness and mythological fantasy and philosophical grandeur of so many other cultures—it may be seen as a collapse of the sublime, an affirmation of unaffected naturalness and simplicity. As in the Tao of Lao-tzu, it is the smile of the child, and the smile of the sage.

It is in this soil, simple, earthy, pragmatic, and humanistic in its most sophisticated forms, that the comic spirit of Zen is rooted, like the lotus flower that radiates from the lowliness of the mud at the bottom of the pond, and whose leaf-pads provide seats for all those little bullfrog Buddhas that are favored in Zen art and poetry. In both

23

its Chinese origins and its later Japanese elaborations, the development of Buddhism known as Ch'an and Zen owes much of its particularity to the distinctiveness of this Chinese and Japanese world-view. Out of the collision of the lofty spiritualism of Indian Buddhism and the earthiness of Oriental humanism and naturalism come both Zen and the comic spirit of Zen. For all of the austerities and rigors of Zen, and the serenity of its religious vision, in it the Chinese dragon smiles and the Indian Buddha roars with laughter.

> *Out from the hollow*
> *Of the Great Buddha's nose*
> *A swallow comes.*

Issa[1]

The Zen tradition, in fact, according to legend, begins with a smile. This in itself, however apocryphal its basis, is a remarkable distinction in the history of religion, and profoundly suggestive of the character of Zen. Insofar as Zen has concerned itself with the question of its lineage, and of its relationship to the historical Buddha and his teachings, it has traced its ancestry not only to the awesome meditation master, Bodhidharma, or to the philosophically formidable figure of Nagarjuna, but to one of the Buddha's disciples, Kasyapa, whose principal distinction is that, at a critical moment, he smiled. According to the tale, when once the Buddha was gathered with his disciples, a Brahma-raja came to him with an offering of a bouquet of sandalwood flowers and requested that he preach a sermon which would summarize his teachings. When the Buddha ascended his customary seat of instruction, however, he did not address the expectant audience, but simply held up a sandalwood flower before the assembly. None of those present understood the Buddha's meaning except for Kasyapa, who received the teaching instantly and acknowledged it with a smile.

This is the peculiar and profoundly symbolic origin attributed to Zen. And it is this smile, this sudden intuition of Truth, and this wordless transmission of the Dharma, that is said to have been handed down through twenty-eight Indian Patriarchs, the last of which was Bodhidharma who brought the doctrineless "teaching" to China a thousand years later (6th c. CE). The Buddha's silent gaze on Vulture

24

Peak is the commencement of that propositionless communication of the innermost nature of things that is pivotal to Zen, that first and last word which cannot be spoken and which cannot be heard. This is the emphasis customarily and not incorrectly given to the Zen use of the legend. Yet the other aspect of the story is also important, and that is Kasyapa's smile of understanding—a smile that is carried through in the subtlest to the most raucous forms throughout the later developments of Zen. This smile is the signature of the sudden realization of the "point," and the joyful approval of its significance. It is the smile of Truth, or the Truth smiling. It is the glad reception of that moment of insight which has taken the whole world by surprise, a moment of seeing with the freshness and immediacy of the little child, full of amazement and wonder—a "holy yea" which is capable of transforming even specks of dust into stars and frogs into Buddhas. It is this smile, historically authentic or not, which is the beginning and the end of Zen.

Bodhidharma and Pu-tai

Insofar as one can speak of fundamental images in a tradition that is so strongly non-symbolic and iconoclastic, there may be said to be two basic types of images in Zen, most noticeable at first in Zen paintings where they are constantly recurring, as if each calls forth and counterbalances the other. One is the epitome of resolute seriousness; the other of buoyant laughter. One is seated in the placid stillness of meditation; the other is airily dancing a folk-dance. One suggests the extremities of earnestness and commitment; the other a light-hearted and carefree playfulness. One presents the visage of the master or sage; the other of the child or clown or fool.

The first set of images in Zen is typified by the figure of Bodhidharma, determinedly facing the wall of a cave for nine years in intense meditation until, according to legend, his legs rotted off. Or Bodhidharma, accepting Hui-k'o as a disciple after the latter had cut off his arm to demonstrate his absolute sincerity and utter seriousness. Or Bodhidharma, confronting all would-be seekers of enlightenment like some fierce and formidable giant whose sheer presence overwhelms the staunchest defences of the ego. Or Bodhidharma, whose piercing eyes shoot forth like daggers from

25

beneath shaggy brows set in a great craggy forehead, seeing through all the schemes of desire and fortresses of ignorance.

The other set of images in Zen is typified by the figure of Pu-tai, the semi-legendary monk of the 10th century, who is even larger in bulk than Bodhidharma, yet more like an overgrown child, and no more awesome and fearsome than the pot-bellied "laughing Buddha" which he becomes. Pu-tai, who refuses to enter a monastery on any basis of permanence, and instead wanders freely without attachment even to the securities of cloistered walls and the forms of monkish discipline. Pu-tai who, like a carefree vagabond, carries a large linen sack from place to place as his only home. Pu-tai, whose jolly, roly-poly figure is to be seen dancing merrily, as if (as in Liang-k'ai's sketch, 13th century) floating gracefully in the air in spite of his size, seeming barely to touch the earth or leave a trace (Plate 3). Pu-tai, whose religious life consists of playing with village children, as if life had now come full circle, as if the end were in some way a return to the beginning, as if even children and fools knew what priests and monks did not.

In consort with the herculean image of Bodhidharma is an impressive train of like figures, such as Lin-chi with his lion's roar, snarling face and clenched fist, shouting and frightening monks directly into Nirvana, as it were. Or Te-shan sitting almost menacingly with his oak-stick poised in his lap, intently awaiting the precise moment when it will be needed for the collapsing of all categories (e.g., the Bodhidharma triptych by Soga Shohaku, 15th century). Similarly, one may point to the two favorite Zen creatures, the tiger and the dragon, which seem to have reincarnated themselves in so many Zen masters, and which, sharing in this same symbolism, serve as powerful animal emblems of the Zen sect.

Yet Pu-tai also has his retinue of attendant "Bodhisattvas" and "totems." And a strange retinue it is. There are the two poet-recluses and monastery fools of the seventh century, Han-shan and Shih-te, with their boisterous, almost mad, and seemingly near-demonic laughter (Plate 1). And there are the three laughing sages of Hu-hsi, overcome with mirth in every painting, as if a Zen trinity were enjoying some eternal joke (Plate 2). Or there is the hermit Ryokan (1758-1831) of the Japanese Soto tradition who, like his Chinese predecessor and counterpart, delighted in playing games with children,

26

or folk-dancing in the village. In fact, so absorbed would Ryokan become in this kind of "zazen" that in one game of hide-and-seek he is reputed to have hid himself with such success under a haystack as not to be discovered until the next morning by a farmer! Furthermore, this set of comic figures has its favorite animals with which it, too, is associated, like the animal vehicles (*vahanas*) of the Hindu gods. But instead of the tiger and dragon, in this case it is the monkey, the frog, the chicken, or even the louse! Liang-k'ai depicts Pu-tai in one painting as deeply and delightedly engrossed in a cock-fight, like a little boy hovering over a crucial game of marbles. Mu-ch'i, in addition to tigers and dragons, featured monkeys, cranes, and swallows. Sengai was fond of frogs. Indeed, one of his frog sketches carries the heterodox inscription: "If by sitting in meditation one becomes a Buddha. . .[then all frogs are Buddhas!]" (Plate 6). Ryokan, among his many peculiarities, devoted special attention to lice, not only giving them a place of honor in his poetry, but sheltering them in his robe. And haiku verse—a literary oddity in itself—under Zen inspiration came to add a motley garden variety of lowly creatures to the sublime objects of aesthetic and religious representation: dogs, geese, and carp; the thrush, the cuckoo, the sparrow, and the crow; yes, and butterflies, fireflies, caterpillars, locusts, ants, bees, and common flies.

> *Sitting like the Buddha,*
> *But bitten by mosquitoes*
> *In my Nirvana.*

Demaru[2]

The tiger is now reduced to a house cat, grinning from the veranda. The dragon is gone, and in his place a dragonfly.

> *He who appears*
> *Before you now is the toad*
> *Of this thicket.*

Issa[3]

The set of images and symbols that cluster about the figure of Bodhidharma have been dealt with extensively in the literature of Zen. Yet what is one to do with this other set of images and symbols,

27

especially when they, and their lowly animal "vehicles," are given such prominence in Zen legend, literature, poetry, and art? What is their function and meaning in this curiously unfolding dialectic? What is it that they reveal? What mysteries do they open up? To what level of being and knowing do they point?

Most of what has been written about Zen, to phrase it as boldly as possible, is Bodhidharma Zen to the virtual exclusion of Pu-tai Zen; or dragon and tiger Zen apart from frog and flea Zen. Only occasionally in some writings, and never at all in others, does this dimension make its appearance and suggest its significance—as if it were only accidentally related to Zen, or perhaps not related at all. In some cases, no doubt, this fairly accurately reflects the character of the Zen of a certain period, or school, or master, or interpreter; and especially when Zen is reduced to an orthodoxy or orthopraxy. Yet the images of Pu-tai, and his strange brethren, and his stranger menagerie of fellow-creatures, right down to the despicable louse, have persisted with the persistence of exhuberant children, chirping crickets, and croaking frogs. In their earthiness and unorthodoxy, their lowliness and commonplaceness, their playfulness and laughter and freedom, they continue to call attention to something very important, perhaps even supremely important, about both Zen and life.

In these terms, a basic Zen question—a koan in its own right—is: What does Pu-tai symbolize? Toward what level of existence, into what kind of spirit, unto what insight and realization, does he, and the odd train of figures that accompany him, like the Pied Pipers of an Oriental carnival, lead?

Half-a-person Zen

It is to be expected that some objection, perhaps even offense, will be taken because of the association suggested here, and frequently made hereafter, between Zen and the clown-figure and the comic-mundane, as if this were making light of, or ridiculing, or debasing Zen. Quite the contrary. This is not to detract or subtract from Zen in the slightest, but rather to add to it that dimension apart from which one is left with only "half-a-person" Zen. Of course, if one understands Zen as simply a "serious business" and therefore sees

28

clown-figures like Pu-tai or Ryokan or Han-shan and Shih-te, as threatening to a Zen so conceived, or if one understands the clown as being a peripheral, shadowy, base, or corrupting figure in relation to the priest or master or seer or sage, then this is correct. Yet there is far more depth and significance, yes, and spirituality in the clown-figure than has commonly been recognized. Clowns, too, belong to a venerable tradition, and have an ancient history, and are no more intrinsically superficial or childish or base than the sacred personages which they often stand over against, parody, and counterbalance. If the clown's function and meaning have suffered many abuses and misunderstandings, so have theirs. If the historical record and actual performance of the clown have often been coarse or demeaning, they are no exception either. Yet at their best and profoundest, clowns, too, can be religious figures and symbols. In this role they stand at least on a par with all other religious personae, and, in some respects, even above them. As in the case of Pu-tai, they may represent a larger spirit and a fuller, more embracing truth. The roundness of Pu-tai is the full circle of existence and the completed vision of life—as in Hakuin's self-portrait in the image of Pu-tai [Frontispiece].

One of the peculiar distinctions of Zen in the history of religion is to have appreciated this possibility, indeed necessity, and to have made it an integral part of the Zen experience and perspective. Among the many unusual—though from the Zen standpoint perfectly normal—features of Zen is precisely that there is a singular and delightful at-homeness of the comic in Zen, and of Zen in the comic, an at-homeness which is surely remarkable and significant enough to be worthy of more extended treatment than it has heretofore been granted. If this appears to be a way into Zen, and a way of Zen, which is strange and uncommon, it must be remembered that Zen masters themselves, as evidenced from the earliest anecdotal records, have often had some strange and uncommon ways of coming into Zen, and of pointing others to it: ways frequently eccentric and unorthodox, nonsensical and clownish, absurd and humorous. A tile falling off the roof and cracking the skull, the ping of a stone striking a stalk of bamboo, a slap in the face or a kick in the chest, a deafening roar or a rollicking guffaw, a single finger held up in silence or an enigmatic barrage of doubletalk: this is but a small sampling of the bizarre

29

techniques and curious occasions for spiritual realization that form the patchwork of Zen history.

What is being alluded to here, then, is not the clown as some inferior species, approaching the infantile or subhuman or chaotic, but the clown who in all lowliness and simplicity and childlikeness, as well as in iconoclasm and a healthy profanity, is truly great, truly profound, truly free. In this sense Pu-tai is a larger image of the Zen-person than Bodhidharma. For his is Bodhidharma having transcended the cave and returned to the light—and, as legend would have it, the very incarnation, in this lowliest of human forms, of the Future Buddha, Maitreya.

Like all mysticisms, Zen is concerned to overcome certain dualities which are seen as splitting up existence, delimiting experience, and hiding true reality. Yet in overcoming such dualities, it is very easy to become caught up, perhaps quite unwittingly, in certain other dualities. These essays are concerned with just such other dualities, in particular those in which the dialectic of Bodhidharma and Pu-tai are involved: seriousness and laughter, sobriety and gaiety, holiness and humor, the dramatic and the comic, commitment and detachment, zealousness and carefreeness, earnestness and disinterestedness, sense and nonsense, purpose and purposelessness, work and play. If the resolution of Zen does not resolve this, then everything has only been resolved into yet another duality, and one is still left with only "half-a-person" Zen.

Defeating the ego, desire, attachment, and discrimination is one thing. Defeating the mentality of seriousness, labor, and the dramatic alone is another—especially when the latter is seen as fundamental not only to the defeat, but also to the marking and maintenance of the victory over the former. If this is all that Zen achieves, then even the little child knows more than Bodhidharma. If this is the terminus of Zen, then even the fool is wiser than the supreme wisdom of the *Prajnaparamita*. If Bodhidharma cannot laugh, it is because he has not seen through his meditation wall. If he cannot play, it is because he is still imprisoned in his cave. If he cannot dance, it is because his legs have indeed rotted off.

The Master's Loud Roaring Laugh

Among the 1700 *koans* which are said to be suitable for precipitating
or deepening an inner spiritual illumination, and also for providing
a test of its genuineness as an awakening, is the following question
attributed to Hsiang-yen, and furnished with commentary by Wu-men
in his 13th-century *Gateless Gate to Zen Experience:*

> (Zen) is like a man up a tree who hangs on a branch by his
> teeth with his hands and feet in the air. A man at the foot
> of the tree asks him, 'What is the point of Bodhidharma's
> coming from the West [i.e., from India to China]?' If he does
> not answer he would seem to evade the question. If he
> answers he would fall to his death. In such a predicament
> what response should be given?

> [Wu-men's commentary and verse:] It is as useless to be
> gifted with a flowing stream of eloquence as to discourse
> on the teaching in the great *Tripitaka*. Whoever answers this
> question correctly can give life to the dead and take life from
> the living. Whoever cannot must wait for the coming of
> Maitreya and ask him.

> *Hsiang-yen is really outrageous.*
> *The poison he brewed spreads everywhere.*
> *It closes the mouths of Zen monks,*
> *And makes their eyes goggle.*[4]

According to the later *Imperial Collection of Ch'an Sayings* (1723-35),
when Hsiang-yen first posed this koan, a leading monk of another
monastery who was present commented: ''I do not ask this question
when the man is on the tree, but I ask it before he climbs up! Will
the Venerable Master speak to this?'' Whereupon Hsiang-yen gave
a loud roar of laughter.[5]

In the elements of humor and laughter visible in such enigmatic
koans and mondos (dialogues) and their witty commentaries or versi-
fied parodies is to be found but one of many examples of the important
place granted to the whole spectrum of the comic in Zen. In Zen,
too, in fact especially, there is a time to laugh and a time to dance,

31

as well as to weep and to mourn (Eccl. 3:4). D.T. Suzuki has argued that "Zen is the only religion or teaching that finds room for laughter."[6] Though in relation to other religions this is, no doubt, an overstatement, in relation to Zen it is more of an understatement. Zen does more than find room for laughter—which might, after all, mean only a very small and rarely occupied room at the back of the house. In a unique sense, the house of Zen *is* the house of laughter. R.H. Blyth, with his penchant for dashing comment and characterization, has defined the essence of Zen as humor.[7] Whether or not one might be satisfied to state the matter so bluntly, such an equation of Zen and humor nevertheless points to the possibility of interpreting Zen as that point in the movement of Buddhism from India to China and Japan in which humor comes to be most fully developed and self-consciously employed as an integral part of both a pedagogical method and an enlightened outlook—that is, both as one of the stratagems for realizing enlightenment and as one of the consequences for enlightenment. Indeed, no more fitting token of this could be found than that of the "loud roaring laughter" for which so many Zen masters have been noted. When a monk asked Shui-lao of Hung, "What is the meaning of Buddha-dharma?" the Master rubbed his palms together and burst into loud laughter. The *Transmission of the Lamp* goes on to report that "this was his normal way of teaching students."[8]

A standard phrase in Zen training, applied to a monk who is so ultra-serious about his disciplines and his "Zennishness" that his very zeal and fanaticism is self-defeating, is that "he stinks (or reeks) of Zen." In the *Transmission of the Lamp* the Indian guru Jayata, who is counted as the twentieth patriarch after Kasyapa, on hearing the diligence of the celebrated Vasubandhu extolled by his followers, criticized him for seeking the Way so earnestly. Said Jayata, "When the string of a musical instrument is too tautly set it will snap."[9]

Over against what is seen here as bondage to earnestness, striving and sincerity, if not a bit of that old demon Pride, stands the commonly repeated phrase in the extensive corpus of Zen anecdotes, with the catharsis and wisdom which it brings: "And the monk (or master) clapped his hands and gave a loud roar of laughter." When Master Kuei-shan sat in evening meditation in the lecture hall, the directing monk came in and beat the fish-shaped wooden drum, snuffed out the lantern, then burst out laughing and clapped his hands. Afterwards the Master asked, "Is there another man like him in the congregation?"[10] Or when Chao-chou asked Master Huan-chung, "What is the essence of wisdom?" the Master repeated the question, as if in echo. Chao-chou burst into peals of laughter and went out. The next day, finding Chao-chou sweeping the yard, the Master demanded, "What is the essence of wisdom?" Chao-chou dropped his broom, burst out with a great guffaw, and clapped his hands in delight.[11]

This is particularly striking when one recalls that the Indian Buddhist scholastics, following the dramatic classifications of Bharata (4th century CE), carefully distinguished between six classes of laughter arranged in hierarchical fashion from the most sublime to the most sensuous and unrefined. Only the most restrained forms were considered appropriate to the comportment of aristocrats and monks, and to the theatrical representation of such. The descending scale of categories itself suggests that the fullest and most pronounced and enjoyable forms of laughter are at the furthest remove from both piety and propriety: *sita*, a faint, almost imperceptible smile manifest in the subtleties of facial expression and countenance alone; *hasita*, a smile involving a slight movement of the lips, and barely revealing the tips of the teeth; *vihasita*, a broad smile accompanied by a modicum of laughter; *upahasita*, accentuated laughter, louder in volume, associated with movements of the head, shoulders and arms; *apahasita*, loud laughter that brings tears; and *atihasita*, the most boisterous, uproarious laughter attended by movements of the entire body (e.g., doubling over in raucous guffawing, convulsions, knee-slapping, and hysterics, "rolling in the aisles").[12]

Given this classification, obviously influenced by the ideals of aristocratic sophistication, it was understood that the first two types represented the restrained, polite laughter of the highly cultured and refined individual; the middle categories, the moderate laughter of the average person; and the last two the intemperate and vulgar laughter of the lower classes. The religious interpretation of this dramatic scheme followed suit, if it did not to some extent influence it. The first two forms approach the spiritual and the sublime; the

33

last two descend into the crassness of the physical and the sensual, lowering and degrading the spirit. As might be expected from the logic of the system, and the presumed threat of laughter with respect to holy things, the Buddha was supposed to have indulged only in *sita*, the most serene, subtle and refined form of laughter.[13] It is almost as if to say that the Buddha was only "guilty" of the first form of laughter!

To the puritanism of the pious imagination, and the humorlessness of the scholastic lack of imagination, it has always seemed unthinkable that the Buddha should have stooped to the barbarous level of openly displaying the teeth in a jovial grin, or of emitting even modest chuckles of amusement, let alone the more immodest forms of hilarity. Yet what is commonly found in Zen, so much so as not only to characterize Zen but to be symbolic of it, is none other than *apahasita* and *atihasita*, the loud, uproarious, unrestrained laughter that is presumably at the furthest distance from the delicate and scarcely detectable smile of the Buddha, and from the placidity that Nirvana represents. As Christmas Humphreys has commented: "There is more honest 'belly laughter' in a Zen monastery than surely in any other religious institution on earth. To laugh is a sign of sanity; and the comic is deliberately used to break up concepts, to release tensions, and to teach what cannot be taught in words. Nonsense is used to point to the beyond of rational sense."[14]

While it may be true at a preliminary level that, as one Japanese *senryu* puts it, "the man who giggles is omitted from the selection for the ambush,"[15] it is also true at another level that those who are incapable of laughter, and of seeing the humor in their situation, are both trapped by their own ambush and omitted from the celebration that follows the ambush. Zen is a kind of ambush undertaken against the traditional Buddhist "devils" of ego, ignorance, desire, attachment, and bondage. But what a strange ambush it is! The peculiarity of the Zen onslaught and surprise is that it is often undertaken in the spirit and with the weapons of the comic rather than the dramatic, in laughter as well as seriousness, and therefore stands from beginning to end within the comic parenthesis. As Yuan-wu commented with respect to a Zen episode which culminated, like so many Zen episodes, in the Master's hearty laugh: "His laughter is like a cool, refreshing breeze passing through the source of all things.''[16]

Thus, while one may be accustomed to seeking for signs of enlightened attainment in the sober features of deep meditation and intense absorption, in Zen one may like as not be presented with images of gaiety, lightheartedness, and mirth. Where we expect a representation of determined resolution and grave demeanor, we are often given instead a picture that seems to suggest profanity more than piety, and frivolity rather than zealousness. When intimations of sublime serenity and unperturbable tranquillity are anticipated, we may in fact be confronted with the raucousness of a laughter that seems to shake the very foundations of the world—which, indeed, is exactly what it does! Zen is not only the tradition of the overwhelming ferociousness of Bodhidharma, who seems to pounce like a great Bengal tiger out of every ink-sketch to break the arms and legs of unsuspecting monks, or like a celebrated Chinese dragon summarily to devour all traces of ego, desire, and attachment. It is also the tradition of the jolly Pu-tai, spurning cloistered confinement, dancing with innocent abandon, and playing with children in the streets, or of the clamorous laughter and mad buffoonery of the monastery fools, Han-shan and Shih-te. Here, too, one discovers that ego, desire, and attachment have a way of getting themselves broken and devoured in the realization of some great Cosmic Joke, and in the greatness of a Cosmic Laughter, which reveals itself in the strange holiness and wisdom of these Holy Fools.

This is, as it were, something of the little comedy that Zen presents in relation to the whole of the Buddhist drama. In fact, the initial impression when confronted with the classical literature and artistic representation of Zen is that one has searched diligently for a spiritual master only to find a figure more akin to a court jester of Mahayana, or has thought oneself to have entered the peaceful repose of the Monastery of Eternal Rest, only to be greeted by shouts and roars seemingly having more affinity with insane or drunken laughter and the blows of a tavern brawl. Bharata's aristocratic and spiritualistic schema seems abruptly to have been stood on its head! Yet it is precisely this entire range of laughter, and the many related categories of nonsense, absurdity, foolishness, playfulness, joking, and humor, that have come to be endowed by Zen with important

35

religious functions and significance, and woven into a remarkable way of perceiving and experiencing life.

There are many things that even the wise fail to do,
While the fool hits the point.
Unexpectedly discovering the way to life in the midst of death,
He bursts out in hearty laughter.

Sengai[17]

CHAPTER THREE

Zen Masters and Clown Figures

> Monk: "During my travels since leaving Chang-an,
> I have never struck anyone with my staff."
> Chao-chou: "That proves that the staff you were
> carrying was too short."
>
> TRANSMISSION OF THE LAMP

One of the first impressions that one receives in reading tales of the often unorthodox lives and ways of many Zen masters is the peculiar correspondence between these figures and that of the clown. Regardless of the problem of authenticity, and the separation of legend from fact, this image is too common and consistent to be dismissed as simply a popular embellishment alien to the character and approach of the Zen master. Whether in part fictional (and therefore still of great symbolic importance) or not, the historical records convey the persistent form of a personality and role to which the designation "clown" is not inappropriate.

This is not to associate the concerns and intentions of Zen transmission with a vaudeville performance, but rather to indicate a level of comic freedom in which the Zen master lived, and the eccentricity of the techniques which he frequently employed, through his own "clownishness" or some humorous artifice, in order to evoke the spiritual awakening and development of his disciples. By odd antics and strange attire, or by crazy sayings and a "divine madness," he gives expression to the special freedom he has attained, and in that freedom reveals some truth through the outlandishness of his behavior.

37

One of the immediate precursors of the Ch'an tradition was Fu Ta-shih, who is said to have been invited by the emperor Liang Wu-ti to expound the *Diamond Sutra*. As soon as he had ascended the seat for his exposition, the emperor listening intently, Fu Ta-shih rapped the table once with a stick and descended from his seat. He thereupon asked the startled emperor, "Does Your Majesty understand?" "I do not!" the incredulous emperor replied. Fu Ta-shih said simply, "The Bodhisattva has finished expounding the sutra."[1] On a later visit it is said that he presented himself at the palace before the emperor wearing a hat, a monk's robe and a pair of shoes, it being accepted practice that a monk wears no hat, a Taoist no shoes, and a layman no monk's robe.[2]

When Master Pao-ch'e was asked what, by the eighth century, had become the proverbial question about the nature of the teaching delivered from India to China by Bodhidharma, Pao-ch'e is said to have stood up, pivoted around on his stick, raised up a leg, and then asked in return, "Do you understand the message?" When the monk did not understand, Pao-ch'e struck him with his stick.[3] Later Kakua, reputedly the first Japanese to study Zen in China, upon returning was requested to address the emperor of Japan concerning all he had learned of this strange sect. Kakua produced a flute from the folds of his robe, blew one short note, bowed politely, and walked out.[4] In stark contrast to the voluminous writings of so many prominent philosophers and theologians, East and West, Kakua reduced truth to this one thing: a single note on the flute.

Aside from the problem of legendary embellishment (or, in this case, abbreviation), the seemingly endless proliferation of like tales in Zen accounts is too conspicuous to be set aside as peripheral to the nature and method of Zen. It is apparent from the host of such anecdotes that have been preserved, and used in subsequent Zen pedagogy, that not only are the early masters depicted as commonly employing various comic techniques in their dealings with monks, laymen, and even local and imperial dignitaries, but as themselves living in the spirit and style of comic freedom. Notorious for their peculiarities and eccentricities, odd in their behavior, and unorthodox in their methods, the Zen masters often suggest something of the trickster, jester, clown, and fool all rolled into one.

The Japanese traveller Ennin, who visited China from 838 to 847, having met Ch'an monks on several occasions, reported that they were "extremely unruly men at heart."[5] Though this appears to be an unsympathetic observation on the part of one who was a member of the T'ien-t'ai (Tendai) sect, and who may have misunderstood and misconstrued what he saw, it points to a trait which is nevertheless there. It is a trait which, in some respects, is reminiscent of that delightful, playful, and sagacious attribute which Lin Yutang called "the old roguery of the Chinese character."[6] In other respects one is reminded of the peculiarities of the early Franciscan monks who claimed an affinity with wandering troubadours and fools, such as Friar Juniper who wore a ragged cowl and was called a blockhead by the people, yet who was seen as having special powers in relation to the Devil, and whose strange antics were accepted as the sign of some special insight and grace. A similar movement is also found among the Holy Fools of the Greek and Russian Orthodox Church: through a divine madness, whether real or affected, they became "fools for Christ's sake" assuming that role as an authentic religious role, and in this way manifesting spirituality through acts of foolishness rather than piety. Selfishness and pride were conquered through an identification with the fool; and through comic exaggerations the folly of the people was dramatized and exposed.[7]

This is not to imply that all Zen masters are clown-figures or holy fools, or that all who achieve awakening within the tradition of Zen do so in the context of comic techniques. Rather attention is being called to a comic spirit and style which achieves its fullest acceptance and development, among Buddhist sects, within Zen, and to a remarkable procession of individualists—one might even say characters—who often appear to be as much at home in the comic as the sacred. In perusing their biographies, and their koans and mondos, one has the impression of being witness to a kind of Buddhist "circus." There is Hsueh-feng who, like the clown that plays at juggling, used to toy with three wooden balls, and who, when a monk would come to him to learn of Zen and the Zen way, would simply begin rolling the balls about.[8] There is Shih-t'ou who, when anyone would ask him to interpret some aspect of Buddhism, would like as not reply, "Shut your mouth! No barking like a dog, please!"[9] There is T'ien-lung who, when Chu-ti, earnestly seeking the true path of the Buddha, solicited his direction, without comment simply lifted up one of his fingers.[10] There is P'u Hua who would clang his meditation bell in the ears of people high and low, aiming to provoke an awakening—though probably seeming only to be provoking. There is Yun-men who would frequently respond, whatever the question, by yelling, "*Kan!*" (No!), and Lin-chi who would shout the meaningless exclamation, "*Kwatz!*" (Ho!).[11] Ma-tsu, also noted for his lion's roar, once shouted so loudly at a disciple that he was deafened for three days—and also thereby enlightened.[12] There is also the case of Tao-lin who was called the "bird-nest master" because he did his zazen seated in the crotch of a pine tree, looking from a distance like a large magpie nest himself.[13]

The *Transmission of the Lamp (Ching Te Ch'uan Teng Lu)*, compiled by Tao-yuan in 1004, is a major source of such information about the early Ch'an masters. Very frankly, and certainly without flattery, it notes the personal idiosyncracies and behavior of notable masters. Of Ma-tsu, for example, the text comments: "His appearance was strange; when he spread his tongue it covered his nose; and he had two wheel-shaped marks on his feet. He walked like an ox, and he looked at things like a tiger."[14] Such statements are doubly remarkable in that they are part of a document being presented to the emperor (Chen-tsung) and by a monk of the Ch'an school.

The same eccentric tradition carries over into Japan, with such figures as Ryokan of the Soto sect. Apparently considered by nearby villagers to be bordering on lunacy, if not over the border, his name literally means "Great Fool." It was he who played with children, and who played with lice. It was also he who, upon being confronted by a burglar in the predicament of being unable to find anything to steal in Ryokan's simple forest hut, apologized to the burglar for not having anything worth taking, gave the man his extra robe, and afterwards composed the poem:

> *A burglar, failing to carry off the moon,*
> *It shines in from the window!*[15]

This motley parade of individuals with their odd behavior and "holy foolishness" seems to file almost endlessly through the voluminous accounts of the Ch'an/Zen masters. Though the purpose is, in a sense, quite serious and the setting acutely authoritarian, nevertheless the panorama has a distinct comic quality intrinsic to it. Through riddles and enigmas, through nonsense and insults, through scowling and laughter, ejaculation and silence, as well as through slapping, kicking and striking, the point is made in, to say the least, a most eccentric manner. It is almost as if one were watching an ancient Oriental version of the slap-stick characters in a Marx brothers film, with the wise-cracking Groucho, the tune-playing Chico, and the wordless Harpo. But, as in all profound comedy, one soon discovers that the object of laughter is really oneself in the larger predicament and folly of humanity.

The familiar self-portrait of Hakuin (1686-1769), the pivotal figure of Japanese Rinzai Zen, is illustrative of the intentional projection on the part of a Zen master of the image of the fool. Hakuin does not sketch himself in the idealized form of an enlightened one, or even in the realistic image of an austere *zenji*, but as a bald, fat, cross-eyed, and hunch-backed old man (Plate 9). The calligraphy Hakuin inscribed above the portrait is even more revealing:

In the realm of the thousand buddhas
He is hated by the thousand buddhas;
  Among the crowd of demons
  He is detested by the crowd of demons.
He crushes the silent-illumination heretics of today,
And massacres the heterodox blind monks of this generation.
  This filthy blind old shavepate
  Adds more foulness [ugliness] still to foulness.[16]

A similar portrait, possibly by a disciple and bearing the same poem, depicts Hakuin as looking almost sheepishly, with pursed lips, out of the corner of his eyes—through all of which, however, one can detect the sagacious twinkle of one who was not easily fooled by sanctimony and pretension.[17] In another sketch Hakuin goes so far as to give his meditating form the unmistakable shape and smirk of the pot-bellied Pu-tai (Frontispiece).

The figure of the clown which stands out here in relation to the

41

person of the master emerges just as clearly in the various tales of Zen monks at the point of death. The classic instance is that of Teng Yin-feng in the eighth century who, when he was about to die, asked, "I have seen monks die sitting and lying, but have any died standing?" "Yes, some," was the reply. "How about upside down?" "Never have we seen such a thing!" Whereupon Teng stood on his head and died. When it was time to carry him to the funeral pyre he remained upside down, to the wonder of those who came to view the remains, and the consternation of those who would dispose of them. Finally his younger sister, a nun, came and grumbling at him said, "When you were alive you took no notice of laws and customs, and even now that you are dead you are making a nuisance of yourself!" And with that she poked him with her finger, felling him with a thud; and the procession carried him away to the crematorium.[18]

In this way Teng, assuming what, from the remarks of his sister, was a not unfamiliar clownishness, expressed his achievement of spiritual freedom, his liberation from a desperate clinging to life and anxiety over self, and therefore his transcendence of the problem of death. What was said by Il Pistoia of the Italian court-fool, Matello, on his death-bed could well be said of Teng Yin-feng: "With him, even Death made sport."[19] There is here an element of both a Promethean laughter in the face of death, and a comic freedom within the larger freedom of enlightenment. The realization of an authentic liberation, as in so much of the Zen tradition, is attested by humor; and the symbol of that liberation is the paradoxical figure of the clown.

The clown in most cultures, in fact, symbolizes emancipation and freedom, even though not necessarily in the most refined or most spiritual sense. Often the antics are simply a retrogressive leap into the irresponsible freedom of the child, or a socially tolerated rebellion against virtue and authority. Partly because of this there is an understandable religious suspicion of the clown, and an attempt to restrict and contain these liberties and profanations. The clown, nevertheless, through the capacity to stand apart from the crowd, its conventions and mores, is a useful symbol, and indeed a herald, of the uninhibited spontaneity and joyful laughter of that spiritual freedom that lies beyond good and evil, not in regression but in transcendence, not in rebelliousness but in emancipation. As Enid Welsford characterized the peculiar role of the clown-fool: "Under the dissolvent influence of his personality the iron network of physical, social and moral law, which enmeshes us from the cradle to the grave, seems—for the moment—negligible as a web of gossamer. The Fool does not lead a revolt against the Law; he lures us into a region of the spirit where, as Lamb would put it, the writ does not run."[20]

In this we are given a hint, at least, as to the basis on which the modern master, Harada Sogaku (1871-1961), lecturing on the text of the third Case of the *Wu-men-kuan*, could direct: "My admonition, then: Be a great fool! You know, don't you, that there was a master who called himself just that [Ryokan]? Now, a petty fool is nothing but a worldling, but a Great Fool is a Buddha. Sakyamuni and Amitabha are themselves Great Fools, are they not?"[21]

If a central characteristic of the fool is foolishness, what defines clowning is a tendency to turn things upside down and behave in a manner opposite to normal expectations. Thereby the clown-figure challenges all those hierarchies that elevate one person above another and those dualities that separate one person from another. The exalted is humbled, and the humbled is exalted; opposites are united, and distances softened. The best modern example of this clownish capacity is Charles Chaplin who, in film after film, played the paradoxical role of the Tramp. The secret of the popularity and profundity of this ambiguous figure was that he was not simply a tramp but a Gentleman-Tramp. Chaplin had ingeniously put together the bowler hat, dress coat, and walking cane of English aristocracy with the baggy pants and floppy shoes of the gutter bum. In this manner he embraced and united in one remarkable individual the top and the bottom of the social order. He was, as Robert Payne said of him, "the whole human comedy wrapped in a single frail envelope of flesh." He became both gentleman and tramp, and neither gentleman nor tramp, and in so doing put the Humpty-Dumpty of our humanity back together again.

From this perspective one may understand the clownish effect of many a Zen anecdote. One day the Prince Governor came to visit Chao-chou, along with royal princes and scholars. Chao-chou, however, remained seated and did not rise in greeting, giving as his excuse for this impropriety a weakness brought on by years of strict vegetarian diet. The next day the prince sent a message to Chao-chou

43

through one of his officers; this time the master rose and came down from his seat to receive him. Afterwards the master's attendant asked why he so politely greeted the officer when he had not even risen to greet the prince. Chao-chou replied: "When a superior class of man comes I deal with him from the Zen seat; when a middle class man comes I get down to deal with him; and for dealings with low class men I step outside the temple gate [to greet them]."[22]

The Wisdom of Children and Fools

The clown-fool is also a favorite motif appearing throughout the history of Zen painting. Two of the most popular subjects are the "Ch'an fools" or "crazy beggars" Han-shan and Shih-te of the early T'ang dynasty. Usually depicted together, as in Yen-hui's diptych of the 12th century [Plate 1], both are represented as holy fools indulging in an hilarious mad-cap laughter—approximating, in fact, the sixth, lowest, most boisterous and presumably un-Buddha-like laughter on the scale of the Indian scholastics. According to Zen accounts, Han-shan and Shih-te had the appearance of tramps, the demeanor of madmen, and the comportment of pranksters. Han-shan is characterized as dressed in tattered clothing, with a nest of birch-bark for a hat, and shoes too large for his feet—the epitome of the clown. Frequently visiting the Kuo-ch'ing monastery at T'ien-t'ai, the temporarily tolerated visitor might be fed with the remnants from the monks' table. And when eventually ushered out of the monastery he would laugh and clap his hands delightedly in a rather ungracious exit, to say the least, by Chinese standards. He is also sometimes represented carrying a blank scroll in his hands, that is, instead of a Buddhist sutra. His friend, Shih-te, whose name means "picked up" and who was apparently an orphan, without name and lineage, also frequented the monastery and was noted for activities equally bizarre. One day, for instance, given menial work to do in the Buddha hall, he was found sitting on the altar with the Buddha image, chatting as if in conversation with an old friend, and sharing in his offering meal.[23]

Outlandish as these comic heroes might appear in either a religious or an artistic setting, as Munsterberg comments, "their carefree

44

behavior and seemingly foolish laughter is characteristic of Zen."[24] A commonly recognized trait of fools is that they are a disguised form of the sage. There is an element of divine inspiration in their apparent madness. A mysterious power is witnessed in the strangeness of their conduct, and some ineffable truth seems hidden in their nonsense. Hence, the familiar acceptance of fools in many societies as being possessed of a spirit, a vehicle for the inbreaking of some supranatural order, attested to by their transcendence of ordinary canons of reason and behavior. A fascinating power is sensed in their presence, which may be a demonic power or a disabling madness, threatening and malevolent, but which may also be a holy spirit and the lunacy of a higher wisdom. Here the babbling nonsense of the fool and the muteness of the mime (like Chu-ti's one-finger-Zen and Han-shan's blank sutra scroll) both "speak" that which cannot be expressed, the truth which is unutterable, and hence are fitting symbols of the "wordless Dharma" which transcends not only all words but all intellectual description and appropriation.

The prevalence of such clown-fools in Zen painting is not accidental, for their unrestrained laughter points to a level of freedom and spontaneity that lies beyond the tensions and dualities of an unenlightened perception of things. The comic spirit and perspective manifest in Han-shan and Shih-te is no ordinary or vulgar hilarity. It represents the achievement of a larger wisdom and a liberation from bondage to ego, ignorance, desire, and attachment. Their peculiarity is not an invitation to eccentricity for its own sake; nor is it a necessary sign of awakening, the imitation of which distinguishes one as an "enlightened one." The idiosyncracies that identify them may or may not be present. Even when they are present they function primarily as symbols of freedom in the highest sense, not just any sort of liberty. They certainly do not provide symbolic justification for the confusion of spiritual freedom with libertinism—the signal for which this has often become outside its original home; for license surely has nothing to do with the rigors and sensitivities of Zen. Random and antinomian behavior, at best, is no more than a regression to childish irresponsibility and self-indulgence—which is hardly what Han-shan and Shih-te represent. Theirs is the Wisdom of Fools that has perceived the true nature of folly.

Another favorite clown-tool in Zen painting is Pu-tai (Hotei), familiar to Westerners as the jolly, pot-bellied, Laughing Buddha readily available in curio shops. As such he is the most popular of the seven gods of luck. Historically he is identified with a wandering priest named Cho Tai-shi (d. 916), who carried a large linen sack (hence the name Pu-tai), which held whatever possessions he had, and also functioned as his sleeping bag. He is usually pictured in the company of children, merry with laughter, and carrying in his linen sack fruits and sweetmeats for the little ones as he travelled from village to village.[25] In two early paintings attributed to Liang-k'ai he is shown in the one bending over, innocently and delightedly watching a cockfight; in the other he is dancing gleefully in playful abandon. As Munsterberg describes him, "the broad face is dominated by the overlarge laughing mouth. . .The upper part of the body is reduced to a big globe-like head grinning above an enormous belly"[26] (Plate 3). He is the dialectical counterpart of the large-headed and heavy-set image of Bodhidharma, with his scowling face and piercing eyes, his beetle-brows and fierce, terrifying countenance.

This relationship between the images of Pu-tai and Bodhidharma is not a playfulness in opposition to discipline and order, and therefore inimical to it, but playfulness which emerges out of the harmony of spontaneity and discipline. It is certainly not the strained or forced frivolity of trying to "have a good time," of pretending to be carefree and spontaneous, or of affecting the image of freedom and gay abandon. It is not laughter over against seriousness and thus in aggressive and hostile tension with it, but laughter in tune with seriousness, and seriousness in tune with laughter. What is being symbolized by the dialectic of the sacred and the comic in Zen is not a new duality, but a new unity, a dynamic rhythmic harmony, as in the first principle of Chinese painting, ch'i-yun (vital harmony, spirit resonance). If the comic spirit provides a contrapuntal effect, as it were, it is not an antagonistic movement, and therefore simply discordant, but an integral part of the unity and wholeness of the composition of life, like the Tao which manifests itself in the inter-relationship between yang and yin.

According to legend, Pu-tai refused the designation of Zen master, as well as monastic restriction, and instead walked the streets with his sack over his shoulder, giving gifts to children, and playing with them in the streets. Sometimes, in fact, he is pictured sitting inside his sack (his only home) impishly peering out. In fair weather he wore wooden clogs (rain-wear) and in the rain he wore straw sandals. Like an Oriental Santa Claus, he was the merry sage with a twinkle in his eye who had rediscovered the wisdom and freedom and laughter of little children. Whenever he met a fellow Zen devotee, he is reputed to have extended his hand, saying in childlike fashion, "Give me a penny." Or if anyone would suggest that he return to a temple or monastery, or more formally instruct others in the Zen path, he would again reply, with an air of innocence, "Give me a penny."[27] Pu-tai represents, therefore, the Zen goal of recovering on a higher plane the spontaneity and naturalness and playfulness—the "little Zen"— of the child. If Han-shan and Shih-te symbolize the Wisdom of Fools, Pu-tai symbolizes the Wisdom of Children. One is reminded of the image of Jesus who paused to play with children, despite his disciples' dismay, or who set a little child in the midst of his all-too-earnest followers with the declaration: "Unless you turn and become like children you will never enter the Kingdom of Heaven" (Matt. 18:3).

It is also significant that Pu-tai, as this strange wandering mendicant, comes to be seen as an *incognito* form of the Future Buddha, Maitreya. The exalted Maitreya manifests himself in the earthly form of the lowly simpleton and fool, "linen-sack." This convergence between the Zen roaring laughter of enlightenment, the mythology of the coming Buddha, and his legendary *avatar*, Pu-tai, is captured in a Buddhist chant about Maitreya:

When the big belly thunders with loud roars of laughter,
Thousands of white lotuses rain through all the worlds.
With his bag of cloth vast is he as the Universe;
He will succeed the Buddha, preaching in Dragon Flower
    Tree Park.[28]

Here, in this remarkable religious chant, Maitreya is given the same comic form in a cosmic setting as that humble figure which he incarnates.

Of similar import is another favorite theme in Zen art, "The Three Laughing Monks at Hu-hsi (Kokei)," treated by painters such as Shih-

47

k'o, Kano, Bunsei, Soga Shohaku, and Sengai. The reference is to the Taoist story of Hui-yuan (331-411) who had, for thirty years, successfully kept a vow never to cross the bridge which separated his monastic retreat at Hu-hsi from the world beyond. But on one occasion, as he was saying goodbye to some fellow hermits who had been visiting him, he inadvertantly crossed the bridge with them. Instead of being upset that Hui-yuan had broken his vow of thirty years, all three began laughing heartily. Su Tung-p'o's words, added to Shih-k'o's version of the scene, capture the epiphany of laughter and, as it were, the Great Cosmic Joke which the jovial trio has suddenly realized: "The three of them are laughing in chorus; even their clothes, hats, shoes all have an amused air. The acolyte behind them is beside himself with laughter."[29] This is not an invitation to laugh at the picture, but with it, to be thrust into the comic dimension of all existence, including one's own.

The clown-motif is, of course, not limited to these commonly represented types, but is extended in Zen painting to a wide variety of subjects and situations: Mu-ch'i's "The Priest Chien-tzu Laughing and Playing with a Shrimp," Soga Shohaku's "Crazy Monk with Frog Hat," Sengai's "Travelling Monk with a Crazy Poem (kyoku)," or Hakuin's "Self-portrait," to name but a few. Similarly, the various other subjects that Hakuin sketched were given much the same touch: the Buddha, Kuan-yin, Bodhidharma, Lin-chi, Daito, and other Zen notables. In addition to their sternness or serenity or gentleness, all seem to participate in and to reveal the comedy of a common humanity, and at the same time to have entered the laughter of the immortals that lie beyond. All suggest that the demons of desire and attachment, ego and ignorance, may be exorcised through laughter, and point to a kind of cosmic laughter that is to be entered on the other side of this exorcism.

This attention paid to the clown-fool in Zen literature and art is especially significant in the light of the Chinese and Japanese emphasis upon reserve, decorum, tranquillity and subdued expression, and a general aversion to extreme displays of gesture and emotion. As Rowley comments with respect to the influence of the Chinese tradition upon canons of subtlety in artistic depiction: "When physical action was required, either in running, playing or fighting, the Chinese

48

resorted to various methods for avoiding the violence of naturalistic portrayal. In children at play, no matter how delightedly they gambol, they look like little men dancing or acting, instead of falling into the rough and tumble of a Western painting. . . Even a drinking bout approximates a discussion among scholars. Only demons, immortals and demon-quellers are permitted to kick and scream and rush madly about."[30] On this scale many Zen masters, painters, and subjects, in their clownishness and foolishness, become the strange bedfellows of demons, immortals, and demon-quellers.

The Zen Artist-Eccentric

George Rowley, in discussing the principles of Chinese painting, makes the oblique comment, which remains undeveloped, that in the Chinese ideal, "the true painter has much of the fool in him. Ku K'ai-chih excelled in buffoonery and Huang Kung-wang called himself the 'Great Taoist Fool'. Painters were expected to be foolish, crazy, cranky or eccentric. . . ."[31] Whether this is an accurate generalization concerning Chinese artists as a whole, certainly it is applicable to the more unorthodox artists classified in the i-p'in (spontaneous, intuitive, untrammelled) category, and to the many like-spirited Zen painters. The eccentricities of many Zen painters and Zen paintings had their roots, not only in the kindred spirit of the Zen masters themselves, but also in the precedent of such pre-Zen Chinese eccentrics as Ku K'ai-chih (4th century CE). In his day it was said of him, "K'ai-chih is compounded half of real madness, half of conscious buffoonery. One cannot understand him without making allowance for both."[32] Of greater importance is the precedent of the subsequent i-p'in artists whose unorthodoxies of manner and technique are frequently matched by unorthodoxies of spirit and life-style.

Of these Wang-hsia (8th century), nicknamed Wang-mo (Ink Wang), is credited with one of the earliest and most unconventional approaches to art. According to Chu Ching-hsuan he was a wanderer with a "wildness of nature" who used wine to creative advantage. "When he was drunk, he would splatter ink on (the surface), laughing and singing the while. He might kick it, or rub it on with his hands, wave (his brush) about or scrub with it...[Then] he would follow its

49

configurations to make mountains, or rocks, or clouds, or water."[33] According to another authority he would even dip his head in the container of ink, and paint with his hair as a brush.[34] Of the same period is a more obscure individual, identifiable only by his family name Ku, who would first lay out dozens of pieces of silk, and after becoming tipsy would run around them, sprinkling ink and then colors. Afterwards he would cover the spots with a large cloth, and with someone sitting on it, would pull it around the room, finally fashioning the blotches and smears into mountains and islands.[35]

Records of other ink-splatterers include Chang Chih-ho, who also imbibed as a preparatory method of releasing inhibitions, and who began by waving a brush over the silk in time to music, with his eyes closed or his head turned away to effect complete randomness;[36] Kuo Chung-shu, who "worked in a style which no master had formed;"[37] and Tse-jen of Yung-chia, who "started out by culling the best points in all the various schools and studying them; then he had a dream in which he swallowed several hundred dragons, after which his achievements were divinely wonderful!"[38]

There is also Chang-tsao "who was able to wield two brushes simultaneously, making with the one a living branch and with the other a decaying trunk."[39] And there is Li Kuei-chen, a wandering individualist, who wore only a single garment summer and winter, and whenever asked about his behavior "would suddenly open his mouth wide and suck his fist, without answering."[40] Of a very different sort is Mi-fei (11th century)—landscape painter, connoisseur, critic, and author of the *Hua-shih* (History of Painting)—who earned the distinction of "crazy (Mi)" for his eccentricities. He is said, for example, to have once dressed in official cap and gown and knelt in a gesture of worship as an expression of his esteem for an unusually beautiful rock.[41] Mi-fei, too, did not favor delicate brushwork or fine silk, but often used the roughest instruments, such as a dry stick of sugar cane, a lotus-stem, or an old rag. He is chiefly noted for his use of dots rather than strokes, achieving the desired effect through an accumulation of dots, applied with a wet brush.[42]

Common to all was the peculiar technique called *p'o-mo* (splashed or spattered ink, including also blowing, wiping, and smearing). The mere representation of forms in an attempted conformity to the lines and colors of the object is downgraded, along with the traditional rules for painting which emphasized technical skill and delicacy of refinement in such representation. These were seen as getting the form and the finesse without necessarily capturing the spirit and entering into the spirit of the subject—indeed becoming one with that spirit. A paramount position is thus accorded the first principle of *ch'i-yun* (vital harmony, spirit resonance) and its intuitive realization and articulation. When Pi-hung asked Chang-tsao who his teacher in the art of painting had been, he replied, "In externals I have taken as my model the creative process of Nature; within, I have the springs of [my own] heart."[43]

As can be seen in this brief summary, the ideas of intuitive grasp and spontaneous expression of the *i-p'in* artistic approach integrate well with the immediacy, simplicity, and naturalness of the *p'o-mo* technique. And both, in turn, synchronize admirably with like emphases in Zen practice and experience. It is no accident that the two traditions, the artistic and the religious, came to find themselves so suited to each other. Though the *i-p'in/p'o-mo* painters hardly represent the dominant image of the Chinese artist, whose painting was much more in conformity with the classical Six Principles advanced by Hsieh-ho (5th century), and whose life-style was more in accord with the Confucian ideal of the gentleman-scholar (*wen-jen*), it is in relation to such unorthodox precursors and contemporaries as this that such early Zen painters as Shih-k'o, Liang-k'ai, and Mu-ch'i are to be seen. Liang-k'ai (13th century) was reported to be "a jocular fellow who called himself 'the crazy Liang'"[44] and also "the crazy vagabond."[45] Mu-chi (13th century), most widely renowned for his "Persimmons," was described—and not particularly with favor—in the *T'u-hui-pao-chien* as "fond of painting dragons, tigers, apes, cranes, wild geese in rushes, landscapes, trees, rocks and human figures; and he did them all in a free and easy fashion, dotting with ink. He expressed his ideas quite simply without ornamental elaboration. His way of painting was coarse and ugly, not in accordance with the ancient rules, nor for refined enjoyment."[46] Shih-k'o of the Five Dynasties Period (906-60) is characterized by a later writer, Liu Tao-ch'un (11th century) in a somewhat different, though no more flattering manner: "He liked to shock and insult people and composed satirical rhymes about them, not unlike those of the comedy actors, some of which are still repeated. . . .He mostly represented old and rustic fellows of strange appearance and grotesque shapes so as to shock the proud and pretentious. The people of Hsi-chou were much annoyed at him. . . ."[47] A similar impression is given in Li Chien's account in the *Hua-p'in* of Shih-k'o's painting of "The Court of the Jade Emperor":

> Shih-k'o was a highly independent character, always mocking and making fun of his contemporaries. His manner of painting was bold and free and he had no consideration for rules and patterns. That is why his figures sometimes are so hideously strange and queer. He painted some of the officials (or divinities) of the Water Palace with crabs and fishes attached to their belts in order to shock the people who looked at them. I have just seen a picture by him, of an old man and woman tasting vinegar; they are holding their noses and squeezing their mouths to show its bitterness. . .In the painting of the Jade Emperor he did not dare to introduce so many playful things [gambolling devils, disrespectful servants, etc.], yet he could not refrain from representing crabs hanging (from the girdles) so as to make people of later times laugh.[48]

Even the presumably serious matter of presenting an official portrait to the master (or, in Hakuin's case, of presenting portraits to himself!), as a token of reverence, esteem and appreciation, is sometimes turned into a comic affair. When a disciple once presented a portrait to Chao-chou, the master responded in koan-like fashion: "If it is really a true image of me, then you can kill me. If it is not, then it should be burned!"[49] The peculiarities of Zen teaching and its occasions seem unending! A different tale is told by P'an-shan, who had requested that a portrait be made of him. Several likenesses were presented to him by his disciples, none of which satisfied him as having captured the spirit of his person and teaching. Then one of his disciples came forward with the assurance that he could do what the others could not; thereupon he turned a somersault and left the room. This was accepted by the master as being the best portrait.[50]

It is often acknowledged that a part of the artist's specific freedom and role as an artist is to stand apart from the conventional masks, the official facades, the socially determined costumes and personae, and thereby perchance to step into and to reveal a more authentic humanity. Being an artist, of course, can also become a social role, with its own masks and costumes and facades, only reduplicating the inauthenticity in another form. Nevertheless the ideal is for the artist to leave a conventional humanity in order to disclose the person behind the person and the world behind the world. This, in itself, places the artist in a curious conspiracy with the clown and fool, a conspiracy in which the artist too may appear as something of a clown or fool. The clown's function is to profane the boundaries and distinctions, the categories and hierarchies, in which we imprison reality and in the same act imprison ourselves. The endowment of all limits and differentiations with seriousness and sacrality is an act of setting things apart, surrounding them with taboos, walling them in their sacred enclosures, setting up "no trespassing" signs—all of which must periodically if not finally be broken through lest they absolutize themselves in a rigidity of forms, and suffocate that which they attempt to preserve.

From the perspective of the clown, who refuses to take any limitations and demarcations with absolute seriousness, the moat that protects the king's castle is also the moat that imprisons the king. Hence, the neat patterns of rationality and order which we use to organize experience are confused and garbled by the clown, whose motley patches, incongruous garb, curious accessories, and bizarre behavior place everything in suspension. Form is turned into chaos, sense into nonsense, inhibition into spontaneity, rigidity into random-ness. The clown does not fit into, indeed refuses to fit into, the patterns and structures of the conventional world, representing some other order of being. The clown gets everything wrong: dress, decorum, logic, speech, gestures, and movements; yet in this wrongness is a rightness of another sort. Out of this foolishness rises another level of wisdom.

It must also be added that, if clowns and fools have a special facility for calling into question the category of the holy, they likewise have a way of not taking the unholy with absolute seriousness either. They go beyond the knowledge of good and evil, sacred and profane— whether the "beyond" that is before or after. As in the figure of the clown-fool in Christendom of the Middle Ages and the Renaissance, though often seen (particularly by ecclesiastical and political authorities) as party to a strange alliance with the Devil and forces of chaos, the demonic realm was also a part of the parody. It is an erroneous belief that the modern clown in Western societies derived from the Devil of the medieval miracle plays. The Devil, too, was dressed in the garb of the clown or fool; evil was placed in the same comic parenthesis as good. If clowns played with holy things, they also played with unholy things. If they dabbled in chaos, they did not do so unambiguously or demoniacally. They entered the no-man's land, as it were, between competing forces of cosmos and chaos, angels and demons, and therefore stood outside both as if both were *maya*, as if both were dramatic yet comic participants in a great stage-play. The clown-fool, therefore, as Enid Welsford argues, was the *punctum indifferens* who existed in a realm beyond both sides of the drama, now seeming to take one side, now another, but ultimately neither: sometimes Vice, sometimes Virtue, yet finally neither Vice nor Virtue.

> This ambiguous position is the inevitable result of the peculiar character of the Fool. The serious hero focuses events, forces issues, and causes catastrophes; but the Fool by his mere presence dissolves events, evades issues, and throws doubt on the finality of fact. The Stage-clown therefore is as naturally detached from the play as the Court-fool is detached from social life; and the fool's most fitting place in literature is as hero of the episodic narrative, or as the voice speaking from without and not from within the dramatic plot. . .
>
> The tragic writer takes this world seriously and interprets it; the comic writer creates a new world, a world where bad people are harmless, where stupid people are merry, where Fate is transformed into a Puck-like Chance strongly biased in favor of those who have a sense of humor and a proper appreciation of cakes and ale. . .
>
> The Fool is an emancipator.[51]

CHAPTER FOUR

Laughing at the Buddhas and Abusing the Patriarchs

When you meet a Buddha, kill the Buddha;
When you meet a Patriarch, kill the Patriarch.

LIN-CHI

The Nirvana Sutra?
This is last in line for cremation.

CHEN LUNG-HSIN

Once when Te-shan visited the temple of Kuei-shan, he walked back and forth in critical examination, only to declare, "There is nothing here," and walked away. The abbot Kuei-shan said of him, "That young man will after this go to some isolated mountain top, establish a hermitage, laugh at the Buddhas, and abuse the Patriarchs."[1] And he did.

There has probably never been a religious movement more sweepingly iconoclastic than Zen. Idols of every sort are relentlessly and mercilessly smashed: not only the ego and its desires and attachments, but scripture, doctrine, tradition, meritorious works, liturgy, prayer, gods, miracles, Bodhisattvas, and even the Buddha himself. Much of the humor in Zen is therefore iconoclastic in character; for before true liberation can occur, all idols must be overturned, or stood upside down. Anything, however holy, is potentially an idol; therefore anything is a legitimate object of laughter. No aspect of one's existence is to be elevated beyond the requirements of humor, including one's existence itself. To take things too seriously, let alone absolutely, however significant they might otherwise seem, is to be dependent upon them and therefore caught in the wheel (the vicious circle) of attachment, desire, and bondage. This is the chain of *karma* and the wheel of *samsara.*

Liang-k'ai's "Sixth Patriarch Tearing Up A Sutra Scroll" (Plate 7) is indicative of the manner in which Zen handles potential idols, and by the same token sources of attachment of every sort, including religious idols. Because anything that is categorized as holy may become simply a new, and more subtle, basis of dependence, instead of a vehicle for emancipation from the bondage of grasping and clinging, holy things must constantly be subjected to profanation. This capacity to profane the sacred, and to do so effectively, yet delightfully—and therefore all the more effectively—is, of course, the special talent of the clown and fool. And the Zen appreciation for, and use of, the techniques of comic profanation is unparalleled in the history of religion and religious art.

Beginning with the first Ch'an Patriarch, Bodhidharma, the comic-iconoclastic motif is central to Zen, as in the tale of his audiences with the emperor Wu-ti of Liang. Wu-ti (465-550) was a very religiously concerned ruler who had expended large sums of money on Confucian temples and schools, and then had turned to Buddhism. Again he spent lavishly for the erection of temples, and for the immigration of thousands of Buddhist priests and monks to teach and disseminate the Buddhist way. For three periods he left his throne to become a monk, only to be coaxed back by his ministers of state—though his days ended during his last seclusion, in the Monastery of Harmonious Peace. In his conversation with Bodhidharma, Wu-ti is reputed to have inquired concerning his accumulation of merit: "Ever since the beginning of my reign I have built so many temples, copied so many sacred books, and supported so many monks and nuns; what do you think my merit might be?" "No merit whatever, sire!" was Bodhidharma's reply.[2]

A similar frankness is amply exhibited in Bodhidharma's successors in the Zen dharma. Master Nan-chu'an was once visited by Chief Minister of the Realm Lu-hsuan, who engaged the master in a discussion of Buddhist themes, Nan-chu'an was clearly not as impressed with the Chief Minister's understanding as was the Chief Minister. When Lu-hsuan said farewell before returning to his administrative office in the castle, Nan-chu'an asked him, "How will you rule the people by going there?" The Chief Minister replied, "I will rule the people by my wisdom." Nan-chu'an responded, "If you do that, the people there may suffer great misery!''[3]

Killing the Buddha

The venerable master Ch'i-lin of Hu Nan province used to enter the Buddha hall and scold the images of the Bodhisattvas Manjusri and Samantabhadra [Bodhisattvas associated with wisdom, meditation, and the monastic path] saying, "You are both devils!" Then he would brandish a wooden sword, pretending to spar with them, and shout, "Surrender!"[4] Similarly, Master Nan-chu'an once announced to his monks: "At midnight last night I gave twenty blows to Manjusri and Samantabhadra and chased them right out of the temple."[5]

Nothing in the entirety of the Buddhist tradition is safe from the iconoclastic fires of Zen, not even the Buddha himself. The classic instance is that of Master Tan-hsia's burning of the Buddha-image. According to the story it was so cold at the mountain temple where Tan-hsia had once stopped for lodging—the snow being so deep that the monks had been unable to get firewood—that Tan-hsia took one of the three wooden images from the altar and used it for firewood (Plate 8). When the horrified chief monk asked him what he thought he was doing, and how he dared profane the sacred image of the Buddha, he replied that he was burning it to obtain its *sarira* (the residue believed left in the ashes of holy persons, providing a potent relic for generations to come). When the chief monk exclaimed, incredulously, "How could a wooden Buddha have any *sarira*?" Tan-hsia replied, "Well, there is no *sarira* so far; why don't we take the other two Buddhas from the altar and burn them too!"[6] Yin-to-lo's (14th century) painting of this episode shows Tan-hsia replying with a pronounced, and somewhat devilish, grin on his face as he warms his hands by the fire. A later depiction by Fugai (1779-1847) brings out the comic-iconoclastic character of the incident in fullest absurdity: the two dominant figures in the sketch are the Buddha-image burning helplessly on the ground, and the pronounced backsides of Tan-hsia as he gleefully warms his bottom over the flames.

In sharp contrast to all recognizable forms of piety and devotion, the Zen records commonly contain profanations of the name of the Buddha. A monk asked Yun-men "What is the Buddha?" His shocking reply: "A wiping-stick of dry dung!" Similarly Te-shan

57

before him had declared, "The Buddha is a dried piece of barbarian dung, and sainthood is only an empty name."[7] Chao-chou once declared, in typical fashion: "The one word I dislike most to hear is 'Buddha'."[8] And Lin-chi offered this characteristic piece of advice to his monks: "Do not take the Buddha for the Ultimate. As I look at him, he is still like the hole in the privy. As to the Bodhisattvas and Arhats, they are all cangues and chains to keep you in bondage . . .Do not deceive yourselves! I care nothing for your expertise in interpreting the sutras (scriptures) and shastras (commentaries), or for your high positions in the world, or for your flowing eloquence, or for your intelligence and wisdom. I only care for your true and authentic insight and perception. Followers of Tao! Even if you were able to expound a hundred sutras and shastras, you would still be no match for a simple and humble monk with no concern for anything."[9]

Once when Lin-chi visited the stupa of Bodhidharma, the guardian monk asked him, "Do you wish to pay your reverence first to the Buddha or first to the Patriarch?" Lin-chi curtly responded, "I do not want to pay my reverence to either!"[10] It was Lin-chi's insistence that one must "kill the Buddha" and "destroy the Patriarchs" in order to achieve liberation and enlightenment; for even the Buddha and the Patriarchs can become a stumbling block to spiritual realization. "Take this mountain monk's advice," taught Lin-chi, "and you can sit on and break the heads of the Sambhogakaya and Nirmanakaya Buddhas. Then you will regard as one of your servants a Bodhisattva of the tenth stage who has completely realized his whole mind; the two forms of supernatural enlightenment will be likened to a cangue worn around the neck of a prisoner; Arhatship and Pratyeka Buddhahood will be likened to ordure in the latrine; and enlightenment and Nirvana to a donkey's tethering stake."[11]

Similarly, when a monk asked Master Teng Yin-feng what were the essential teachings of the Buddha and the Patriarchs, he retorted: "The Buddha is a bull-headed jail-keeper, and the Patriarchs are horse-faced old maids!"[12] The more recent master, Sengai, who produced a number of comic sketches, had the audacity to paint his own death scene with himself sitting in the hallowed place of the Buddha in the traditional *Parinirvana* scene. It was also Sengai who was responsible for the incredible, by usual religious standards, sketch of a small boy

leaning over to relieve himself of intestinal gas, with the accompanying title, "The One Hundred Days Teaching of the Dharma."
This and many similar pieces of iconoclastic literature and art, comically profaning the whole gamut of Buddhism from the Buddha on down, take on additional significance when one recalls the more popular level of Mahayanist piety that invaded China, as reflected in such a work as the *Butsu Myoko* (Sutra of the Names of the Buddha). Translated into Chinese by the 7th century CE, it comprised twelve volumes providing the faithful with the names of no less than eleven thousand and ninety-three Buddhas and Bodhisattvas, the recital of which assuredly brought peace, prosperity, purgation of sins, merit, and ultimately Bodhisattvahood.[13] Pure Land advocate Tao-ch'o (562-645) in his *An-le-chi* (Book of Peace and Happiness) argues, in fact, "Is it not said that even once thinking of Amitabha Buddha and uttering his name cleanses us from all our sins committed while transmigrating for eighty billion kalpas? If even one thought achieves this, how much more if one constantly thinks of the Buddha and repents one's [sinful deeds]!"[14] Yet when a monk asked Master Ta-kuan whether he ever performed the *Nembutsu* (repetition of the invocation to Amida Buddha, *Namu-Amida-Butsu*), he replied, "No, I never do!" "Why not?" "Because I am afraid of polluting my mouth!"[15]

The tenor of much of Mahayanist piety, in dialectical relation to which Zen stands as if almost completely divested of all religious sentiment, is expressed in a hymn of the 11th century:

Ah! Pity it is we cannot see the Buddha face to face,
Though He is present always, everywhere.
And yet, perchance, as in a vision, He will come to us
In the calm morning hours, when no man stirs.[16]

Relative to this much of Zen seems insensitive, impudent, and irreverent, if not blasphemous, as in the boldness of Ikkyu's (1394-1481) lines:

Sakyamuni,
That mischievous creature,
Having appeared in this world –

59

How many, many people, alas,
Have been misled by him![17]

Or in another of Ikkyu's poems he writes:

Why are people called Buddhas after they die?
Because they don't grumble any more,
Because they don't make a nuisance of themselves![18]

If Zen stands, as it does, within this larger Mahayanist tradition, it does so most iconoclastically; and this iconoclasm is central to Zen from its earliest patriarchal period, contemporaneous with such texts as the *An-le-chi* and the *Butsu Myoko*, into the modern period.

Burning the Sutras and Shastras

According to the *Transmission of the Lamp*, after the Buddha had taught the dharma for forty-nine years and had "transmitted the lamp" to Kasyapa, the Buddha said, "The original dharma of all dharmas in no-dharma."[19]

With the Zen emphasis upon the "wordless Dharma" it is no surprise to find that the Buddhist sutras and their commentaries receive their fair share of (symbolic and literal) tearing and burning. Han-shan carries a blank sutra scroll, Hui-neng tears up a sutra scroll, and Te-shan and Hsiang-yen burn all their sutras and shastras. The statement of Yun-men may be taken as representative of Zen iconoclasm with respect to scripture: "What a mess are the Three Vehicles [the *Triyana*], the teaching of the twelve divisions of the Canon, and Bodhidharma's coming from the West! Is it not advisable to let it pass; and if it is not allowed to pass, is it worth a single shout?"[20] Or there is the case of Yang-shan who was asked by his master Kuei-shan: "Of the forty books of the *Nirvana Sutra*, how much might be ascribed to what was spoken by the Buddha and how much to the speech of devils?" Yang-shan answered, "It is all devilish talk." Kuei-shan remarked, "From now on, there will be no one who can correct your opinion."[21]

The dangers of overdoing such an iconoclasm in relation to scripture are, of course, those of losing valuable points of reference, turning freedom into license, and confusing ignorance with wisdom.

No doubt this occurred in varying degrees in the hands of lesser monks and lay disciples. As one contemporary critic of early Ch'an argued: "The harm done from depending too much on the sutras and philosophical treatises is slight compared with the harm from positively ignoring them—an attack which is a great hindrance to properly following the Buddhist life." The same author, a member of the rival T'ien-t'ai sect, cites the lament of another critic of Zen: "The worst part of it is, indeed, that those ignorant villagers, after visiting the Zen monasteries and listening to sermons given by the masters, are inordinately delighted, and without giving much thought to the spirit of the teaching, declare themselves to be teachers, not only disparaging the ancient worthies but depreciating the sutras and their contents with their own incoherent utterances."[22]

No doubt Zen did play into the hands of an antinomianism and anti-intellectualism which simply failed to make the distinction between non-attachment and either cavalier disregard or blind ignorance. The risks in such thoroughgoing iconoclasm are very real, and should not be minimized. Ridicule can easily become an end in itself, or a subtle technique of rationalization, going nowhere, destroying, and putting nothing in its place. It can easily be exploited as a justification for indolence, or for regression to childish forms of impulsive behavior, obeying only the whims of the moment. On the other hand, any method is subject to misuse and misinterpretation, and one must assume that the Zen masters were as aware of the problem as their critics. Such seems to be intimated in the comment of Yang-shan that those coming to him received, and could only be given, what they were seeking: "Shih-t'ou keeps a shop dealing in solid gold only, but mine handles a variety of wares. If a man comes for a rat's droppings, I let him have them. If he wants solid gold, I also meet his wish."[23]

Tai-hui makes clear the necessity of mediating between extremes in his letter to a disciple: "There are two forms of error now prevailing among followers of Zen, laymen as well as monks. The one thinks that there are wonderful things hidden in words and phrases, and those who hold this view try to learn many words and phrases. The second goes to the other extreme forgetting that words are the pointing finger, showing one where to locate the moon. . .They reject all verbal teachings and simply sit with eyes closed. letting down the eyebrows as if they were completely dead."²⁴ Both are forms of attachment and bondage; therefore, both must be subjected to iconoclasm. I-tuan, a disciple of Nan-ch'uan, expressed the matter more simply and epigrammatically to his assembly: "Speech is blasphemy, silence a lie. Above speech and silence there is a way out."²⁵

The defense of Zen's "tearing and burning" scripture is put in a characteristic manner by Tai-chu: "Awakened to reality, they throw away the doctrine, just as a fisherman, having caught his fish, pays no more attention to his nets; or as a hunter, after catching his rabbit, forgets about his snare."²⁶ A millenium earlier Chuang-tzu had written much the same:

> *The purpose of words is to convey ideas;*
> *When the ideas are grasped, the words are forgotten.*
> *Where can I find a man who has forgotten words?*
> *He is the man I would like to talk to.*²⁷

But this is all from the standpoint of having caught the game, or located the moon. Thus, the same Lin-chi that kills Buddhas and Patriarchs, and discards sutras and shastras in favor of a good shout, also insists that "only a greatly enlightened person dares to slander the Buddha and Patriarchs, criticize people all over the country, repudiate the teaching of the *Tripitaka*, and insult and humiliate small lads and those who want to seek something in favorable or adverse circumstances."²⁸

Zen Parody of Zen

Given, however, the Zen attitude toward, and use of, scripture, this only added to the crucial importance of the masters themselves, their own spiritual realizations, their ability to communicate them, and to evoke, guide, and test such in their disciples. All of this opened up another potential source of dependence and attachment, much like that of a modern patient in relation to a psychoanalyst. The "wordless Dharma" also demanded a different sort of authentic transmission than that of scriptural texts. In order to verify the legitimacy of Zen as a Buddhist sect, and to establish its authenticity in relation to the challenges of rival sects, certain Zen enthusiasts as early as the eighth century had worked out a direct line of apostolic succession through

33 patriarchs, 28 of them Indian and 6 (counting Bodhidharma both ways) Chinese, to which was later added the legend of the Buddha's transmission of the silent teaching to the smiling Kasyapa. Though Zen might successfully, therefore, avoid attachment to scripture and creed, and dependence upon verbal teachings and rational arguments, its result might be only that of establishing a new form of attachment and dependence in relation to the Zen master himself. While undoubtedly there were those who succumbed to this temptation, it is to the credit of Zen masters and disciples alike that the same comic iconoclasm which they turned toward all other forms of bondage was also commonly turned toward the master, the patriarchs, and the apostolic succession as well. This, in itself, to say the least, is an unusual phenomenon in the history of religions. The goal of the master was to kill the disciple and the goal of the disciple was to kill the master.

A classic instance of this is to be found in Shu-an's preface to Wu-men's *Gateless Gate to Zen Experience*, the 48 cases of which have served as a basic Zen text since the 13th century:

> If it be said that there is no gate by which to enter Zen, everyone on earth will enter by it; and if it be said that there is a gate, our master will find no ground on which to erect this (gateless gate to Zen experience).
>
> He has commented thoroughly on the text from beginning to end, and this is like putting one hat on top of another.
>
> I am urged to praise this book (by writing a preface). This, again, is as foolish as crushing a dry bamboo to get juice.
>
> When one happens on a book of this kind, he is well advised to throw it away without waiting for the advice of an old man like myself, who would do just that. . .[29]

As if the point were not sufficiently underlined by the preface, and by Wu-men's commentary and verse on the text—which is often as humorous and iconoclastic as the preface—an appendix of the same order is offered as a forty-ninth case by the scholar-statesman and Zen adept, Amban:

> The venerable Wu men made the words of forty-eight

63

cases, and judged the ancient worthies' koans. He is like a fried-bean-cake seller. The buyers have their mouths opened and the cakes pushed in until they are full, and they can neither swallow them nor disgorge them. That is what it is like. But Amban wants to add another extra cake. . .I don't know where the Roshi will put his teeth into it. If he can swallow it, he will emit light and move the earth. If he cannot, I will fry them all up together again.[30]

This inner-directed iconoclasm is also illustrated in the way in which so many collections of cases of koans, mondos, and anecdotes from earlier masters are commonly handled by the later master who edits them, or re-edits them by freely reinterpreting them, perhaps rejecting the earlier interpretation or use of the materials, or the behavior of the previous master on such and such an occasion. This approach, epitomized in Wu-men's commentary and verse in the *Wu-men-kuan*, and the "hat piled upon hat" of the preface and appendix, is referred to as *nenro*, meaning "to pick up and play" with the master's materials, often humorously parodying his words and ridiculing his actions. Even the verbal and behavioral heritage of the master is not sacrosanct. The contrast with the warnings that often accompany sacred texts and utterances, such as that which concludes the Christian *Revelation of St. John*, is striking indeed:

I warn every one who hears the words of the prophecy of this book: if any one adds to them, God will add to him the plagues described in this book; and if any one takes away from the words of the book of this prophecy, God will take away his share in the tree of life and in the holy city, which are described in this book.[31]

Any attempt, likewise, at developing and defending a philosophical or doctrinal orthodoxy, even under the claim of representing a Zen philosophy and doctrine, is submitted to the iconoclastic fires of Zen. The Zen inclination is constantly to burn its own scriptures and commentaries. In one Zen tale visiting monks at Fa-yen's temple were arguing over the philosophical questions of the relationship of mind to reality, attempting to apply the teachings of scriptures and masters to the problem. Fa-yen interrupted with the question, "Here is a large boulder. Do you say that it is inside or outside your mind?" One of the monks confidently hastened what he took to be the orthodox reply: "From the Buddhist viewpoint everything is an objectification of mind, so that I would have to say that the stone is inside my mind." "Your head," quipped Fa-yen, "must be very heavy."[32]

On the other hand, even Zen as a meditational discipline and practice, however much it may suggest itself as essential to Zen as Zen (i.e., as the very meaning of the term, deriving from the Sanskrit, *dhyana*, meditation), and as crucial to the "wordless Dharma," must not be permitted to absolutize itself as method or form. Otherwise Zen has only exchanged an orthodoxy for an orthopraxy, and therefore a new point of attachment and dependence. What is critical, finally, is not the particular technique used, for all techniques are one or another form of *upaya* (accommodating method). Success, or lack of success, cannot be attributed only to the method. As Huai-jang responded to a monk's question on the right thing to do to become a Buddha, "If the ox-cart will not move forward, which should be beaten, the cart or the ox?" He then went on to advise: "In learning sitting-in-meditation, do you aspire to learn the sitting Ch'an or to imitate the sitting Buddha? If the former, Ch'an does not consist in sitting or in lying down. If the latter, the Buddha has no fixed postures. The Dharma goes on forever, and never abides in anything. You must not therefore be attached to nor abandon any particular phase of it. To sit yourself into Buddha is to kill the Buddha. To be attached to the sitting posture is to fail to comprehend the essential principle."[33]

Perhaps the most sacrosanct element in Zen, then, is the stress on the "wordless Dharma," faithfully transmitted from the Buddha through the patriarchs, and summarized in the so-called "Zen creed" attributed to Nan-chu'an:

> *A special transmission outside the scriptures;*
> *No dependence upon words and letters,*
> *Direct pointing at the soul [inner being] of man;*
> *Seeing into one's nature, and the attainment of*
> *Buddhahood.*[34]

Yet there are instances of both the transmission and the teaching being

65

parodied, as in Wu-men's commentary on the legend:

A long time ago when the World Honored One was dwelling on Vulture Peak, he picked up a flower and showed it to the congregation. They all remained unmoved, but the venerable Mahakasyapa smiled. The Honored One said: "I have in my hand the doctrine of the right Dharma which is birthless and deathless, the true form of no-form and a great mystery. It is the message of non-dependence upon words and letters and is transmitted outside the scriptures. I now hand it to Mahakasyapa."

[Wu-men's commentary]: Golden-faced Gautama behaved outrageously. He reduced the sublime to the simple. He sold dog meat for mutton and thought it wonderful to do so. Had the whole congregation smiled, to whom would he have transmitted the right Dharma? Had Mahakasyapa not smiled, to whom would he have transmitted it? If you say that the right Dharma can be transmitted, the golden-faced old man deceived the world. If it cannot be, how could he give the message to Mahakasyapa?

> When he held up a flower
> His secret was revealed.
> When Mahakasyapa smiled
> No one in heaven or on earth
> knew what to make of it. [35]

The fate of Bodhidharma, revered founding father of the Ch'an school and symbol of so much in Zen, is no different. Wu-men's commentary on the forty-first case of Zen "teaching" is no less iconoclastic:

The broken-toothed barbarian [Bodhidharma] came hundreds of thousands of miles (!) across the sea proudly [to China], seeming to stir up waves on a windless day. Later he instructed a pupil and crippled him [Hui-k'o]. Alas, the fisherman does not know his ABC's.

> A direct message from the West [India]
> Is in this story:

The troublemaker for Zen monasteries
Is you, the guilty one [Bodhidharma]. [36]

Perhaps it is not entirely inappropriate to Bodhidharma's character and the character of Zen that, based on the legend of his meditation for nine years facing the wall of a cave until his legs rotted out from under him, he later became the humorous Japanese daruma doll—as well as a snowman for Japanese children. The comical pear-shaped figure has no legs, and, like the invincible clown, however toppled over, stands up again. [37] An old Japanese *senryu* adds the final *reductio ad absurdum:*

> *In another hundred years,*
> *Only Daruma's head would have been left.* [38]

Even the most sacred moments of Zen experience are not exempt from comic profanation and the humbling qualifications of humor, as in the episode of the enlightenment of Tung-shan. The story is one of four cases given by Tai-hui in a letter of advice to his disciple, Lu Chi-i. In the exuberance over his awakening, Tung-shan had exclaimed to his master, Yun-men: "After this I shall build my little hut where there is no human habitation; not a grain of rice will be kept in my pantry, not a stalk of vegetable will be growing on my farm. And yet I will abundantly treat all the visitors to my hermitage from all parts of the world; and I will even draw off all the nails and screws of their attachment. I will make them part with their greasy hats and ill-smelling clothes, so that they are thoroughly cleansed of dirt and become worthy monks." Yun-men twitted him: "What a large mouth you have for a body no larger than a coconut!" [39] Yun-men was quick to detect a potential reversion to egoistic pride, and the possibility of a new idolatry, in the zealous compassion of a fledgling Bodhisattva who was now self-assuredly about to enter the fanaticism of saving the whole world.

In Zen iconoclasm the relationship between the sacred and the comic is really the same as in all polarities that stand in dialectical relationship. It is a dialectic which both heightens the tension and annuls it, bringing it into a higher and profounder unity on that plane of experience in which both elements are transcended and brought to fulfillment. This is captured so well in Anagarika Govinda's charming description of the juxtaposition of sacred dancers and ritual clowns in Tibetan Buddhist mystery plays. The primary participants in the ceremony are the gorgeously costumed and fantastically masked representatives of Buddhas, superhuman saints, and celestial and demoniacal beings. They are the very personification of the sacred and sublime relative to the profane and the ordinary. But as these "awe-inspiring figures solemnly wheel around, the almost unbearable tension and exaltation, which has gripped the spectators, is suddenly relieved by the appearance of two grotesquely grinning masks, whose bearers are aping the movements of the sacred dancers, and seem to mock the Buddhas and even the terrifying Defenders of the Faith. They are weaving in and out of the solemn circle, gaping into the faces of the dancers, as if defying and ridiculing both the divine and the demoniacal powers. These, however, seem to take no notice and move on with unperturbed dignity. The effect is astonishing: far from destroying the atmosphere of wonder and sacredness, the juxtaposition of the sublime and the ridiculous rather seems to deepen the sense of reality, in which the highest and the lowest have their place and condition each other, thus giving perspective and proportion to our conception of the world and of ourselves."[40]

This, in much less dramatic and ritualized form, is the place of iconoclasm in Zen. Veneration and profanation, reverence and irreverence, profound respect and equally profound parody, are united in such a way that the total effect is not discord but an alerting dissonance, not a chaotic cacophony but a dynamic rhythmic harmony. "By experiencing opposite poles of reality simultaneously, we actually intensify them. They are like the counterpoints in a musical composition. . .Seriousness and a sense of humour do not exclude each other; on the contrary, they constitute and indicate the fullness and completeness of human experience, and the capacity to see the relativity of all things and all truths and especially of our own position."[41]

CHAPTER FIVE

The Buddha and the Bullfrog

An old pond.
A frog jumps in.
Plop!

BASHO

Santayana argues that at the heart of comedy lies a confusion of categories ordinarily kept distinct, like applying the formulae of theology to cookery or of cookery to theology.[1] Comedy is therefore a trespasser upon the holy ground of spheres which we expend a great deal of energy in defining and keeping separate, only to have them thrown back precipitously into the same knapsack with odd bits of everything. The king is forcibly tossed by the court jester into the street with the beggar. The Bodhisattva is suddenly indistinguishable from the novice monk. Gods and goddesses are made to consort with common animals. And the Buddha is placed in the lotus pond along with the frogs.

This is the comedy of the scroll-scenes (*choju-giga*, or animal caricatures), traditionally assigned to Toba-sojo (1053-1140), in which monkeys, foxes, rabbits and frogs take the place of monks, priests and laymen in Buddhist ceremonies, as well as in a variety of secular activities. In one of the delightful culminating scenes of the first scroll, a monkey officiates as head priest in a temple service, praying before the altar of a large bullfrog Buddha seated on a "lotus" throne made of cabbage leaves[2] (Plate 5). Though these are not Zen sketches—Toba-sojo having been an abbot of the T'ien-t'ai (Tendai) sect—they are of the same order as many Zen works and serve to indicate that Zen was not alone in its appreciation for the importance of the comic perspective both religiously and aesthetically.[3] In Zen, however, the employment of this dialectic is more consistent throughout its history, more central to the tradition, and often more radical. In correspondence with the thorough-going iconoclastic temper of Zen is an equally thorough-going emphasis upon the earthy, the ordinary, and the everyday, which constantly manifests itself in Zen literature, art, and life.

The Collapse of the Sublime

Dating from the ninth and tenth centuries in China, Zen painting, like Zen literature, instruction, meditational practice and monastic life, marks a distinct break from the typical, Indian-inspired, Mahayanist Buddhist themes, scenes, and subjects. As Osvald Siren comments, Zen painting generally "had very slight, if any, connection with traditional forms of Buddhist art."[4] In place of the glorified and exalted Buddhas and Bodhisattvas, elegantly and royally attired, awesomely displaying their superhuman powers and surrounded by a host of heavenly beings and lesser spirits, are the extremely plain, down-to-earth, unmistakably human sketches of the Buddha, Bodhisattvas, Arhats, and various Zen masters and patriarchs. The figures are often very powerfully represented, as in the numerous portrayals of the founder, Bodhidharma. But it is a very this-worldly power, immediately open to the self-realization of all men, and the total effect is that of very simple and mundane figures.

The "portraits" of Bodhidharma, or even Sakyamuni himself, are the antithesis of the magnificent imagery familiar from early Chinese caves such as Tun-huang and Yun-kang,[5] or early Japanese temples like Horyuji[6]: Amitabha (Amida), the Savior-Buddha, beckoning from the paradisaic splendor of his Pure Land; Kuan-yin (Kannon), patron of mercy with a thousand arms of compassion, and the seemingly endless multitude of other benevolent Bodhisattvas, offering their treasuries of grace and merit; or Maitreya (Miroku), the Future Buddha, holding forth the promise of his coming dispensation. As Suzuki put it with respect to the transformation of Mahayanist figures in Zen: "Both Kannon and Monju [Manjusri, Bodhisattva of Wisdom] were brought down to the market or the woods or anywhere we humans were accessible. Kannon was pictured with a basket filled with fish; Monju came out to our world accompanied by the monkey or the crane."[7]

R.G. Collingwood argues in his aesthetics that "the theory of laughter belongs to the philosophy of art; the satisfaction which we find in it is an aesthetic satisfaction, and to this extent the comic is a form of the beautiful. . .A mere collapse or disappointment is not comic; it must be an aesthetic collapse, a collapse of the sublime."[8] Zen art hardly signals a disappointment, but it definitely signals a collapse of the sublime, and does so both aesthetically and religiously. This is the reason—or one of the reasons—why the comic spirit and perspective is so much at home in Zen and Zen art; for one of the functions of comedy is to bring everything back to earth, if need be by making things fall into the mud. The very juxtaposition of the gorgeous, heavenly Buddhas, arrayed in their radiant power and glory, seated in lavishly decorated and richly adorned Buddha-fields, with the perfectly plain and unpretentiously humble figure of Bodhidharma facing the wall of his cave (Sesshu), or of the Fifth Ch'an Patriarch carrying his hoe (Mu-ch'i), or the Sixth Patriarch bending over, cutting a stalk of bamboo (Liang-k'ai), is itself comic, quite apart from any specific inclusion of comic motifs.

This is just as true whether one takes the type of portrait that becomes official from the 13th century on, in which Bodhidharma is pictured as burly, stern and awesome, with heavy brows and piercing eyes, and a visage suggestive of a tiger or dragon, or the slight, rather ordinary, and more compassionate-appearing patriarch found in the manuscript illustrations of the *Chuan-fa-cheng-tsung* (ca. 1054 CE) and the palace roll of figures painted by Chang Sheng-wen (ca. 1176 CE)—although the former treatment tends more toward caricature and lends itself more to comic subtleties.[9] In either case, as Suzuki puts it, Zen "took away from Buddhist figures that aloof, unconcerned, rather unapproachable air which had hitherto characterized them. They came down from the transcendental pedestal to mingle with us common beings and with common animals and plants, rocks and mountains."[10] The divine became human, as it were, in its peculiarly mundane Zen form as the dimension of Buddha-nature (*Buddhata*) in all human beings, indeed in all things.

The radicalism of the Zen transformation is even more striking when compared with the magnificent imagery of the Mahayanist sutras, which provide the literary counterparts of such artistic splendor and profusion. In a Pure Land sutra, for example, the wondrous form of Amitabha is offered to the devotee as an object of contemplation:

> His body is colored like the pure gold in a hundred, a thousand, ten thousand, and a hundred thousand Yama-lokas [Yama heavens], (with the height of) as many yojanas as there are sand grains in six hundred thousand lacs of nayutas [millions] of Ganges rivers. The white hair between his eyebrows curls five times to the right like five Mount Sumerus. His eyes are like the water of four oceans with the blue and white clearly distinguish-able. The pores of his body send out rays of light as great as a Mount Sumeru. The halo (round his head) contains a hundred lacs of great chiliocosms [billion worlds] wherein appear Nirmanakaya Buddhas as many as there are sandgrains in a million lacs of nayutas of Ganges rivers. Each Nirmanakaya Buddha has a following of countless Transformation Bodhisattvas serving him. Amitayus Buddha has 84,000 marks; each mark has 84,000 excellent characteristics; each characteristic sends out 84,000 rays of light; and each ray of light illumines and attracts to it all living beings in all worlds in the ten directions who (earnestly) think of him.[11]

In relation to this fabulous immensity and dazzling brilliance, the Zen treatments of the Buddhas and Bodhisattvas, insofar as they are treated at all, appear as if starkly and nakedly human, abruptly and uncere-moniously stripped, as it were, of all mythical fantasy, regal splendor, and preternatural glory. As Suzuki says of the equally marvellous Buddha of the *Gandavyuka*: "He no more sits on a high seat decorated with seven kinds of jewels, discoursing on such abstract subjects as Non-ego, Emptiness, or Mind-only. On the contrary, he takes up a spade in his hands, tills the ground, sows seeds, and garners the harvest. In outward appearances he cannot be distinguished from a commoner whom we meet on the farm, in the street, or in the office . . .The Buddha in his Chinese Zen life does not carry his *Gandavyuka* atmosphere ostentatiously about him but quietly within him."[12]

The same inversion occurs with respect to other orthodox Buddhist themes and scenes. In place of a depiction of the fabulous episodes from the *Jataka* tales of the Buddha and his 499 previous incarnations, or the profusion of myths associated with the cosmic deeds and realms of a host of other Buddhas and Bodhisattvas, or the variety of levels and tortures in Buddhist hells and the correspondingly extravagant Paradise scenarios, Zen painting, like Zen literature, offers the this-worldly landscapes and commonplace events of everyday life: Ma-yuan's "Old Man Asleep in a Boat," "Man Fishing," or his "Monks Playing Chess in a Bamboo Grove" (12-13th century); Liang-k'ai's "Sixth Patriarch Cutting Bamboo," or his "Monk Eating Pig's Head" and "Monk Playing with a Shrimp" (13th century); Mu-chi's "Monkeys," "Swallows," and "Persimmons," or his "Priest Sewing his Mantle" (13th century); Yu-chien's "Mountain Village in Clearing Mist" (13th century); Mo-kuan's "Four Sleepers" and "Kingfisher" (14th century); or Josetsu's "Fishing for a Catfish with a Gourd" (15th century). This not only reflects a movement away from stock religious themes and pious devotional images—Buddhas, Bodhisattvas, gods and goddesses, monsters and demons, legendary episodes—but the admission of almost any aspect of existence as a legitimate religious theme and artistic subject. The sacred cosmos is "profaned" in order that the sacredness of the "profane" world might be revealed.

This is not to suggest that the conventional Mahayanist motifs are never treated by Zen artists. But they are certainly no longer dominant motifs, and even when they are treated it is in a distinctly this-worldly, concrete, and ordinary-human manner. As in Ch'en-hsien's (17th century) illustrations of Sakyamuni, Kuan-yin, Arhats, monks and priests, the treatment does not, as Siren puts it, "always seem to be as reverential as the traditional motifs might imply. . .[he] has transformed the saintly men into ordinary human beings divested of their holiness."[13] In Suzuki's words, "The Chinese practical genius has brought the Buddha down again on earth so that he can work among us with his back bare and his forehead streaked with sweat and covered with mud. Compared with the exalted figure at Jetavana surrounded and adored by the Bodhisattvas from the ten quarters of the world, what a caricature this old donkey-leading woman-Buddha of Shou-shan, or that robust sinewy bare-footed runner of Chih-men!"[14]

The same may be said of the Mahayanist paradises, as exemplified in the magnificent murals of Horyuji, which present the four paradises of the four directions, with Sakyamuni's paradise in the south, Amitabha's in the west, Bhaisajyaguru's in the east, and Maitreya's in the north.[15] Paradise, for Zen, is immediately accessible and is indistinguishable from the world of ordinary perception—though not as ordinarily perceived. It is not to be located in some other world, nor in a world which one enters by closing the eyes and shutting out the mundane and the commonplace, nor a world which by its holiness and infinity and brilliance devalues this world, empties it, and renders it impure, drab, and profane. It is not the world at the end of the rainbow of fantasy and mind-expansion, or at the furthest remove from this world. As in the T'ang master Yen-yang's characterization of such Buddhist fundamentals as the Three Jewels (Buddha, Dharma, and Sangha) and the corresponding Three Refuges ('I take refuge in the Buddha; I take refuge in the Dharma; I take refuge in the Sangha'), it is the world in which "the Buddha is a mass of clay, the Dharma is the moving earth, and the Sangha is one who eats gruel and rice!"[16] Or as Eicho commented, referring to the contemplative image of the the Buddha's spiritual body (*Sambhogakaya*) as golden in color and sixteen feet in height: "Zen makes a humble blade of grass act as the Buddha-body sixteen feet high, and, conversely, the Buddha-body sixteen feet high act as a humble blade of grass."[17]

If one moves from subject matter to style, the same mundaneness and unpretentiousness is evident. The Zen style, so clearly reflected in the techniques and effects which it utilizes, is not the extravagant, the luxurious, the ornamented, nor the riotous display of lines and colors, nor the seemingly endless proliferation of subjects and objects filling every particle of space, but the plain, unadorned, suggestively sketchy strokes of the brush, the aversion to detail—let alone adornment—and the impressionistic capture of moments of fleeting experience. In relation to the extravaganzas of Mahayanist art which had made its way into China from India, Zen art represents a determined refusal to indulge in the embellishments and profusions of mythological fantasy or the ornateness and splendor of the pious imagination, hardly in fact even to indulge in coloration at all, with its decision to return, most frequently, to the earlier, non-Buddhist, Chinese monochromatic tradition of painting, stemming from calligraphy, and its favoring of the unorthodox *i-p'in* style and *p'o-*

mo techniques.[18]

Whether it is in terms of subject matter or style, therefore, it is the kind of art world in which, as it were, court jesters are much more at home than their kings and queens, buffoons than their lords and ladies, and in which priests and devotees look more out of place than clowns and fools, or for that matter than birds, fish, and frogs. It is the kind of world in which Hakuin can sketch a scene of a Zen priest urinating, or Sengai offer his "One Hundred Days Teaching of the Dharma," which features a boy leaning over farting! It is the kind of world in which it is not inappropriate for both Hakuin and Sengai to accompany their works with "crazy verses" or for Sengai to substitute himself for the Buddha on his deathbed in the most sacred *Parinirvana* scene. Lest this should appear to be an example of a low point in Buddhist spirituality, it must be remembered that Hakuin was one of the most significant and prominent masters in the history of Japanese Zen, and that Sengai, a noted master in his own right, was only giving expression in ink and verse to an unusually profound appreciation for the significance and sacrality of even the lowliest and most "profane" aspects of life. When confronted with such individuals it is easy to react, as does Munsterberg, with the customary misgivings of aestheticians and religionists when faced with similar phenomena: "It is on this note that Zen painting drew to its close—a note of gaiety and charm, no doubt reflecting the decline which Zen had suffered in modern Japan."[19] One might just as well have said, "reflecting the decline which brought Zen into being," i.e., the collapse of the sublime.

Overcoming Sacred and Profane

So thorough-going is this collapse of the sublime that it has been seen by some interpreters as the result of secularizing tendencies, either in Chinese culture in general or Zen in particular. It is to be acknowledged that there are certain historical realities which have had some part to play in this shift. The various persecutions of Buddhists, the most devastating of which was that of Emperor Wu-tsung in the years 842-45, when it is said that 40,000 Buddhist temples were destroyed and 260,000 monks and nuns forced to resume lay life, were misfortunes which a radical Zen iconoclasm, and a Zen incorporation of much of the Chinese outlook and sensibility, were exceptionally well-suited to weathering. Zen itself was not unrelated to the corresponding resurgence of an emphasis upon indigenous Chinese thought and culture, with its distinctively this-worldly and humanistic character, over against alien forms of Indian spirituality. In dealing with Zen, one must pay special tribute to the very practical, realistic, and moderate character of the traditional Chinese philosophy of life, which would not accept Buddhism apart from a stress upon the mundane and the human. High-flown metaphysics and extended forays into other-worldly spheres of pious speculation and yearning must often have appeared as "much ado about nothing" before the realism and common sense of the Chinese perspective, informed as it was by both Confucianism and Taoism. In Hu Shih's well-known description of the context out of which Zen emerged: "The Chinese mentality is practical and abhors metaphysical speculation. All the religions and philosophies of ancient China were free from the fantastic imaginativeness and hair-splitting analysis and gigantic architectonic structure which characterize all religious and philosophical literature in India. When China was brought face to face with India, China was overwhelmed, dazzled and dumbfounded by the vast output of the religious zeal and genius of the Indian nation. China acknowledged its defeat and was completely conquered. But after a few centuries of bewilderment and enthusiasm, the Chinese mentality gradually reasserted itself and began to search for those things which it could really understand and accept. It now undertook to sift from this vast literature of Buddhism those elements which might be regarded as essentials in distinction from the impressive images and grandiose rituals and unintelligible metaphysics and superstitious charms and spells."[20]

This is not to say that mythological and legendary materials are completely absent in Zen. The substantial first section of the *Transmission of the Lamp* offers a good deal of such material in tracing the history of the Zen tradition, beginning with seven Buddhas prior to the historical Buddha, and proceeding through twenty-seven Indian patriarchs. The death scene of the twenty-seventh patriarch Prajnatara, for example, reads as follows: "Having transmitted the dharma, the Master stood up on his seat, stretched his hands, left and right, and radiated from each of them twenty-seven rainbow-colored beams of light. He then raised his body in the air to the height of seven palm trees and transformed it by fire, cremating his own body. The *sarira* fell down like rain from heaven. A stupa for them [the granules of *sarira* collected as holy relics] was built in the first year of Ta Ming (457 C.E.)."[21]

What is significant is that Prajnatara is the last Indian master before Bodhidharma who brought Zen to China. In the *Transmission* the preponderance of mythological and legendary material is found in conjunction with these early stories of Indian patriarchs. They are "the sort of thing" that tended to come from Indian Mahayana and that tended to be associated with India. The stories of the Chinese patriarchs are much more down-to-earth and no-nonsense (or with a lot of apparent non-sense). While not without legendary traces now and then, they give the strong impression of believably human and historical figures engaged in daily life, whose dialogues and deeds have an air of authenticity rather than fantasy about them.

The kind of secularity and humanism and good-humored matter-of-factness that has always graced Chinese culture, and that is early manifest in such a delightful manner in Chuang-tzu, is now manifest in the happy marriage of Taoism with its Chinese dowry and Buddhism with its Indian legacy, the offspring of which is Zen. "There is no question that the kind of thought and culture represented by Chuang-tzu was what transformed highly speculative Indian Buddhism into the humorous, iconoclastic, and totally practical kind of Buddhism that was to flourish in China and Japan in the various schools of Zen."[22] This Chinese contribution to Zen of the mundane and the comic is illustrated, perhaps as well as by anything, in Lin Yutang's comment that "Chinese scholars always bequeath to us so many collections of 'notebooks'. . .consisting of unclassified paragraphs, in which opinions on the authorship of literary works and corrections of errors in historical records are mixed up with accounts of Siamese twins, fox spirits and sketches of a red-bearded hero or a centipede-eating recluse."[23] This is very much, in fact, an apt description of what a collection of Zen paintings or Zen anecdotes looks like.

Chinese art and literature, generally, reflects a devoted attention to the endless variety of this-worldly objects, a congeniality to even the lowliest creatures and most common particulars of day-to-day existence. The whole range of earthly life is opened up as if, in itself, a sacred mystery, as if in its very miscellaneousness the proper locus of reverent attention, and as if the true paradise, realistically perceived, were to be found in the beauty and refined awareness of the "Pure Land" immediately available to experience. The most cursory glance at a collection of Chinese, as well as specifically Zen, paintings, or a skimming of the classical records and accounts, reveals the same detailed surveillance of the menagerie of ordinary delights. There is Chang Seng-yu who is remembered for his snow scenes; Chou-fang for his court ladies; Pien-luan for his birds and flowers. Han-kan excelled in horses, Chang-hsuan in women and girls, Han-huang in oxen, Tai-sung and Tai-i in buffaloes. Feng Shao-cheng is noted for his dragons and birds, Sun-wei for his dragons and turbulent water. Li Ai-chih's specialty was cats. Hsu-hsi's forte lay in flowers, butterflies, and garden vegetables, including cabbages; Mei Hsing-ssu's was barnyard fowl. Prince Chun was eulogized for his treatment of bamboo, and also as a "clever painter of shrimps," while the prince of Chiang-tu was acknowledged as an "expert painter of sparrows, cicadas, and donkeys." Ch'i-tan was at his best in "the hairpins and hatstrings of the Court," and Fa-shih in "picnicking noblemen." K'uai-lien was especially fond of cranes, and Ts'ui-k'o remarkably captured the subtle distinctions between hares.[24]

The recognition that Zen adopts rather than creates this climate does not, however, in the least depreciate the contribution of Zen itself; for the primary context of Zen was still religious and Buddhist. In relation to the established conventions and treatments of this tradition, Zen self-consciously turned away to more "secular," mundane, and comic forms of art and literature. To be sure, there is here a kind of secularization process at work in Zen, which on one side is a purging of holy things and lofty compositions of their special sanctity and sublimity. Yet at the same time this process takes place in a religious context, and involves a sanctification of its own: the sacrilizing of the earthy, the human, the commonplace event, the "meanest creature and flower." As in the practice, dating from the earliest Zen monasticism, the master meditates and teaches and guides; but he also participates, like everyone else, in building, cultivation, cooking, sweeping, and washing. The one activity is not sacred, and the other secular; rather, the distinction has been transcended. Indeed, particularly from the viewpoint of the Southern (Sudden Enlightenment) School, it is just as possible to achieve enlightenment in the act of cleaning as in meditating or studying the sutras.

There is, of course, the story of the prominent 11th-century painter, Li Lung-mien, who was warned by a (Ch'an?) monk[25] that if he continued to paint so many horses he would be reborn as a horse, whereafter, it is said, he began to deal with more obviously religious themes! As the evidence suggests that he nevertheless continued to paint horses, and other "secular" matters, in his later years, the anecdote either originated in a jest or was the apocryphal invention of a Buddhist attempt to situate his religious works in his mature years.[26] Even in dealing with religious themes, however, Li was apparently instrumental in mellowing and further humanizing the earlier manner of representing Arhats (which was in itself quite this-worldly), softening the severity and grimness of their features, replacing the "rather terrifying old men with their ravaged and foreign [Indian] features. . .by more pleasant-looking, well-nourished monks of a rather jovial appearance."[27]

This perspective is also aided by the grand Mahayanist theme of the universality of Buddha-nature (*Buddhata*). The Buddha-nature, that is, is not in some beings or places rather than others. Of the various schools of Mahayana, Zen seems to have excelled in going out of its way to call attention to what some of the lowlier of these beings and places might be. The Buddha-nature is not only to be found in the heavens but on earth, and not only on earth but in earthworms. One of the dialogues in the *Transmission of the Lamp* shows a monk questioning Master Ching-ch'en on the subject. Though he begins his questioning at the lofty level of Bodhisattvas, Buddha-realms and Buddha-dharmas, he ends up discussing earthworms. The question to which he finally comes is: "When an earthworm is cut in two pieces, both pieces move. In which half does its Buddha-nature dwell?" The master does not protest the sudden intrusion of earthworms, but simply replies, "(Tell me) what realm is moving, and where is the immovable?"[28]

The effect of the Zen achievement is not secularization as such, but a kind of spiritual democratization of things in which the categories of importance versus unimportance, value and valuelessness, profundity and triviality, wisdom and simplicity, beauty and ugliness, good and evil, sacred and profane, no longer apply. Or, to put it more positively, it is a revaluation of things in which the distance between great and small, lofty and lowly, powerful and weak, magnificent and plain, extraordinary and common is reduced to nothing, permitting a magnanimousness of spirit in which even the humblest and poorest and dullest of creatures is seen as having its own significance and value. The exalted is humbled, and the humble is exalted, as it were. A dualistic way of thinking which arranges things and compares things and separates things, and which interposes its classifications between the experiencer and the experienced, is toppled. As Master Kuei-shan remarked: "When all feelings about the saintly and the profane have been wiped out, there will be exposed the body of true eternity."[29] In the same way Hui-neng instructed his disciples: "If someone asks you about the meaning of existence, answer him in terms of non-existence. If he asks about the worldly, speak of the saintly. If he asks of the saintly, speak of the worldly."[30]

Such a perspective can, of course, be viewed as a very serious and sobering one. Yet, like the collapse of the sublime, it is also at the heart of the comic perspective. The clown and the comedian have often functioned at their best as the great levellers in relation to all hierarchies and all distinctions, however sacred. Through overturning, or puncturing, or collapsing, or standing things upside down, they effect a reversal or flattening of categories and discriminations, the result of which is closely akin to that sense of unity and fellow-feeling, that oneness or identity of all things that mystical experience realizes. It is in this sense, too, that Zen masters and artists have commonly performed the clown's role in relation to and within the larger Mahayana tradition. If the dualities and oppositions such as beauty and ugliness, sacred and profane, truth and error, are seen as a part of the spiritual problem, it has always been a primary function of the clown and the fool to annul just such distinctions by reducing the sublime to the ridiculous, profaning the sacred, turning reason into nonsense, and giving the prize to the ugliest man in town. Theirs is the Emersonian motto: "I unsettle all things. No facts are

80

to me sacred, none are profane." The precious gem is treated as a common pebble, while the common pebble is fondled as a precious gem.

The mystical goal of bringing about a collapse of categories, curious as it may seem at first sight, is also the intent of the comic spirit. In some respects it intensifies the categories and contrasts as a mock-prelude to collapsing them. The beauty is placed with the beast, the king is made to walk hand-in-hand with the beggar, the wise man and the village fool are put side-by-side in the seats of honor, and the Buddha and the bullfrog are placed on adjacent pads in the lotus pool. Such a mystical integration of opposites is already prefigured in the body-paint and costume of the clown in so many cultures, an amalgamation which sets together white and black, order and disorder, symmetry and asymmetry, finery and patchwork, fastidiousness and dishevelment, royal insignia and peasant attire. It is the separation and yet coincidence of Tweedledum and Tweedledee, the juxtaposition-in-unity of the baggy pants and undersize coat of a Charlie Chaplin, or the clumsied gracefulness of many a clown. It is the circus fat lady paired off with the thin man, the beautiful maiden parading with the ugly dwarf, or the graceful trapeze artist soaring above the stumbling imitations of the clown in the ring below. The mystical *coincidentia oppositorum* is symbolically achieved in the motley figure and the *punctum indifferens* of the clown-fool. His is an amorphousness and an ambiguity that represents an order of being and knowing that lies before and beyond all duality and hierarchy, in that region of freedom and innocence and playful spontaneity attained only by little children and great sages.

The Recovery of Simplicity

Parallel to this movement in Zen art is a similar collapse of the sacred and the sublime in Zen literature, almost in fact a collapse of literature itself, with the Zen preference for anecdotes and abbreviated discourse, if not simply shouts and exclamations. A comparison of the incredibly profuse productivity of the Mahayanist literature introduced into China, in addition to the extensive Theravada *Tripitaka*, with the sparse and minimal production and use of literature in Zen, is most significant. Mahayanist sutras are even more effusive in both prodigality and fantastic content than Mahayanist art, which certainly attempts, but is physically unable, to more than hint at the colossal proportions and stupendous numerations of the Mahayanist visionary imagination. Mahayanist literature opens up like an unending and inexhaustible treasurehouse of spiritual delicacies, in relation to which Zen seems to stand like a small plot of arid scrub-land to an infinity of cosmic jungles.

In place of the monumental *Mahaprajnaparamita Sutra*, for example, with its 600 fascicles, Zen uses the brief *Hridaya* (heart) epitomization of the great sutra, which in its Chinese translation by Hsuan-chuang contains only 262 characters. Similarly the massiveness and luxuriance of the *Saddharmapundarika* and the *Avatamsaka* stand in stark contrast to the explosive abruptness of Chao-chou's "*Wu!*" or Lin-chi's "*Kwatz!*" It is as if one had been invited to a sumptuous banquet table in a great hall, expecting to be gorged on a seemingly endless feast of choice meats and rare delights, only to find beneath the elegant lid of the great silver serving platter the crisp remains of a common sparrow. In fact, this is the suggestion of an anecdote told of Master Fa-yen. He was about to deliver a discourse to his waiting monks, but upon ascending the platform he heard the twittering of a swallow outside the assembly hall; whereupon he remarked, "What a profound discourse on Reality, and a clear exposition of the Dharma!" and descended from the platform.[31] Here the accolades of Mahayanist piety in the *Amitabha Buddha Sutra* are brought to a most straightforward fulfillment: "Streams, birds, and trees are all chanting Buddha and Dharma."

The Japanese haiku, too, frequently associated with and used by Zen, is a fascinating instance of this same emphasis upon the common and the simple. The haiku is sublime in its very aversion to the sublime, and magnificent in its insistence upon being completely bereft of adornment. Clothed in the plainest and most modest garment of but seventeen syllables, and using only the most everyday elements for its subject matter, it is a poetry that only a culture with a devoted attention to the most trifling particulars, and an unusual sense of the comic, could have imagined.

On the temple bell
Perching, sleeps
The butterfly. Oh![32]

There are, of course, some haikus which are overtly humorous, as this one by Buson, or Issa's lines:

Yes, the young sparrows
If you treat them tenderly
Thank you with droppings.[33]

Yet the haiku itself is a comic achievement; for when confronted with that which would require an infinity of words to express, it proposes to restrict itself to the very least intelligible number. Offering itself thus as the most exquisite and purest form of poetry, it has only a beggar's display of the most mundane experiences and everyday objects, immediately accessible to anyone.

On a withered branch
A crow has settled—
Autumn nightfall.
Basho

New Year's Day:
Clouds dispersed, and sparrows
Chattering away
Ransetu[34]

The haiku presents, as a special gift, what all people everywhere have in their possession at all times!

There is also a sense in which—as unrelated as the two may seem—one may even speak of a collapse of the sublime and the sacred in Zen meditational practice. Again the larger Mahayanist context must be kept in view. According to the Pure Land meditation manual, *Amitayus Dhyana Sutra*, there are sixteen subjects of contemplation given by the Buddha to aid the devotees of Amitabha in visualizing and ultimately attaining the glories of rebirth in his Western Paradise: the setting sun, pure water, the ground of Paradise, its jewelled trees, its merit-giving water, its jewelled palaces and heavenly music, its gem- and pearl-studded lotus throne, the three Holy Ones, the radiant body of Amitabha, the golden body of Avalokitesvara, the golden body of Mahasthamaprapta, Amitabha's realm of bliss, the bliss of the three Holy Ones, the inferior class of rebirth in Paradise, the middle class of rebirth, and the superior class of rebirth. In each step of the elaborate progression, the devotees are to saturate their minds with, and be elevated by, the stupendous and overwhelming images that are offered to the imagination—as in the tenth stage of contemplation, which is directed to the golden body of Avalokitesvara:

(His) golden body reaches the height of 800,000 lacs of nayutas [millions] of yojanas [distance of a day's march], with an *usnisa* [cranial protuberance of a Buddha], and a halo around his neck. His face, *usnisa* and halo are each a hundred and a thousand yojanas high. Within the halo there are five hundred Nirmanakaya Buddhas who look like Sakyamuni Buddha. Each Nirmanakaya Buddha has a following of five hundred transformation Bodhisattvas together with an incalculable number of devas who serve him. . .The Bodhisattva's face is of golden hue and between his eyebrows a curl of seven colours emits rays of 84,000 kinds of light. Inside each ray there is a countless number of Nirmanakaya Buddhas. Each Buddha is surrounded by an incalculable number of Transformation Bodhisattvas who serve him and reproduce at will all the transformations that fill all the worlds in the ten directions. . .The Bodhisattva's palms are colored like five hundred lacs of many hued lotus. Each finger tip has 84,000 lines as (clear as) if they had been printed thereon. Each line has 84,000 hues each of which sends out 84,000 rays of soft light which illumine everything. With these precious hands he receives and delivers living beings.[35]

The meditational practices of Zen stand in much the same kind of relationship to such contemplative luxuriance as does Zen in relation to the larger portion of such Mahayanist literature, art, and piety. Zen meditation is not meditation *on* something, let alone an infinitely expanding horizon of holy things. Nor is it contemplation attempting to soar on phantom wings to ever more grandiose and supernatural heights. The distinguishing mark of zazen is its utter simplicity. It does not proceed by filling the mind with an incalculable parade of images, however glorious and edifying, but by emptying the mind of all objects of attachment. It is the utter simplicity of *sunyata* (Emptiness), which is not mere emptiness, but emptiness of the clutter of objects of desire and clinging, even holy desires and a clinging to sacred things. It is an emptiness wherein lies all fullness, a fullness which comes not through filling the mind to overflowing but through emptying it, and hence opening it in the widest manner possible.

The first time one is introduced to Zen meditation one searches about for something on which to contemplate. The mind furtively dances, like the monkey that it is, about the meditation hall in the frantic hope of finding something to do, some object to fix itself upon and hold to. Impatiently one waits for the show to begin, for the ritual to be performed and the sermon to be preached, for some treasury of myth and symbol to be opened up, for someone at least to say something or do something. But the show never begins. No lesson is given; no land of enchantment is offered; no edifying thought is developed; not even any background music or interlude is provided to shield one from the silence. Nothing happens. One is confronted only with bare walls, the minimum of ritual, and the silence of emptiness, interrupted only by the awakening and alerting blows of the *keisaku*.

This is not, however, the substitution of a mere nothingness for the bewildering profuseness of Pure Land contemplation. *Sunyata* is not a quantitative but a qualitative emptiness. The possibility of such a misunderstanding is provided with a typically Zen corrective in K'uo-an's 12th-century meditational drawings, with commentary, of the Ten Bulls, based on the earlier Taoist Eight Bulls. The Taoist sequence had symbolized the culmination of the search for Truth and Reality by an empty frame, representing the Nothingness beyond both object (bull) and self (man). K'uo-an, however, added two more scenes which rescued the progression from what might have been construed as a termination in the dead end of a barren nothingness. His ninth scene, "Reaching the Source," depicts a tree, a bird, and a stream with fish; while the tenth, that of "In the World," depicts a monk approaching a child, and "mingling with the people of the world" (Plate 10). Another line of K'uo-an's commentary reads, "I go to the marketplace with my wine bottle and return home with my staff."

This escape from a sterile, if not abstract, emptiness is what is also so clearly seen in the popular figure of Pu-tai, dancing or playing with the village children—of which K'uo-an's tenth scene is reminiscent. Insofar as pictures are appropriate at all, the picture which best symbolizes the Zen experience of emptiness, and the context of that experience, is not the empty frame, but the ordinary world of trees and birds and fish, the world of shops and wine bottles and walking-sticks, seen now through, and in, the experience of *sunyata*. As Shan-neng put it: "We must not cling to the wind and moon of the day and ignore the eternal Void; neither should we cling to the eternal Void and give no attention to the wind and moon of the day."[36]

Like the world of the comic spirit and perspective, which also has its way of returning everything to the Source and to the World, Zen brings everything back down, not only from a mythic other-worldliness, but from a vacuous emptiness, down to the very humble and unpretentious level of mingling with people, going to the market place, and returning home. As Chia-shan once remarked to his disciples: "You should perceive this old monk in the tips of the grass, and recognize the son of heaven in a crowded market."[37] The point is similarly expressed as the achievement of the fifth and highest stage in Tung-shan Shou-ch'u's (10th century) schematized path of enlightenment:

Lo, he has arrived at supreme unity!
Beyond the "is" and the "is not,"
Who dares to follow the rhymes of his poetry?
Let others aspire to the extraordinary!
He is happy to return home and sit amidst ashes.[38]

As Alan Watts has suggested, "according to Zen, the reason why our quest for some ultimate reality is so difficult is that we are looking in obscure places for what is out in broad daylight."[39] What is needed is not a closing of the eyes, or some dazzling psychedelic vision, but their opening to the reality that stands plainly and nakedly before us and within us. The only requirement is the very difficult, yet perfectly simple and natural, one of seeing things as they are apart from the filter of categories, without the interposition of value judgements or thoughts of possession and use—without even the enhancement of some symbolic aura or mythic coloration. It is to see the world and the self in that isness or suchness, that emptiness, which lies behind and beyond all words, all estimations of value and purpose, all symbols and myths. These serve to cloak reality in the very act of attempting to mediate and clarify it. Thus when a novice asked Master Chaochou, "I have just entered the brotherhood and am anxious to learn the first principle of Zen. Will you please teach it to me?" Chaochou responded, "Have you eaten your supper?" The novice replied, "I have." "Then go wash your bowl!"[40]

It must be said, nevertheless, in all fairness, that the incredibly sublime visions of so much Mahayanist art, literature, and meditation, if not taken literally but as highly symbolic profusions of imagery, may be seen to be pointing, in their own fantastic and allegorical way, to many of the same insights as are to be found in Zen. As Suzuki points out, such motifs as the intricate interrelatedness of all things, the interpenetration of the most infinitesimal particle and the totality, the profound sense of inscrutable mystery, and the realization of the presence of the whole in its meanest part, are already there in the Mahayanist tradition, but now intuited by Zen in the most plain, straightforward, and no-nonsense manner.[41] They are reached in Zen, not through a fabulous display of fantasy which runs the risk of simply swelling the imagination and boggling the mind, but through a complete elimination of all marvels and embellishments in an effort to move directly to the heart of the manner: as in the laying aside of the 600 fascicles of the *Mahaprajnaparamita Sutra* for a concentration upon the bare 262 characters of the *Hridaya* (heart) of the sutra, or the reduction of the entire scriptural corpus, as it were, to a single "*Kwatz!*"

There is a definite dialectical relationship here between the two Buddhist poles represented by Pure Land and Zen of the sublime and the common-mundane, the fantastic and the ordinary, the infinitely complex and esoteric and the utterly simple and obvious. The Zen emphasis does not stand alone; rather it has meaning in the larger context of the Great Vehicle of Mahayana. The very acts of profanation and inversion involve an element of relationship and interdependence. Any impact derives in part from the force of its counterpart, and exists relative to it, just as the point of a joke cannot be made unless at least a modicum of its opposite (seriousness and rationality) precedes it. Like the opposition and yet harmony of the *yang* and the *yin* in relation to the Tao, the sublime and the simple are relative perspectives which counterbalance and complement each other, which are in tension and yet in harmony, and whose harmony moves into that higher harmony that is the Tao or the Dharmakaya itself. Both in their own ways point toward the ultimate mystery of being, the one by the overpowering majesty of its images, the other by the amazing simplicity, the incredible poverty, of its forms.

CHAPTER SIX

The Celebration of the Commonplace

Drinking tea, eating rice,
Passing time as it comes;
Looking down at the stream,
Looking up at the mountain...

PAO-TZU

It is commonly asserted that the Chinese and Japanese are basically a non-religious people, at least as judged by Western or Indian standards. Certainly there is an emphasis upon the pragmatic, the human, the everyday and the this-worldly, and a relative lack of interest in metaphysical speculation, theological formulation, mythological vision and devotional liturgy. Certainly also the term *aesthetics* often seems more appropriate than the term *religion*, and the finest expressions of the Oriental spirit culminate in art and poetry rather than in myth and ritual or religious philosophy. If emphasis is laid, however, upon a sensitivity to ultimate mystery, where religion and art necessarily meet, then the Chinese and Japanese in their profound appreciation of this *mysterium* in poetry and painting are as religious as any. Here we encounter that fundamental level of experience which lies behind and within all experience, even the most ordinary and commonplace, and in which the inexhaustible mystery of being manifests itself to human consciousness.

What is particularly intriguing, in fact, is that whereas many peoples tend to locate this experience in certain unusual, if not "supernatural" moments and circumstances out of which it is evoked, the Oriental focus is upon mystery in the most obvious, ordinary, mundane—the most natural—situations of life. In the words of the Ch'an master, Yuan-wu, "One particle of dust is raised, and the great earth lies therein; one flower blooms, and the universe rises with it."[1]

Everyday-mindedness

The terms used by Yuan-wu derive from a Mahayanist text, the *Gandavyuka*, in which the wondrous power of the Buddha is seen as manifest in his ability to interpenetrate all phenomena, so that the tiniest particle contains the entirety of the whole:

> All this is because he has the miraculous power of transforming his one body and making it pervade the entire universe...It is because he has the miraculous power of manifesting all images of the Dharmadhata within one single particle of dust; it is because he has the miraculous power of revealing all the Buddhas of the past with their successive doings within a single pore of his skin.[2]

Though it is to this theme that Yuan-wu alludes, his use of it is quite different. It is as different as the search for the miraculous in some ethereal realm beyond the world of the everyday, and the realization of the miraculousness that is to be found in the everyday world itself, whether in a single particle of dust or a single pore of skin. The colossal world of the Indian *Gandavyuka* has been stood on its head. It is not a matter of the Buddha engaged in miraculous metamorphoses, manifesting the entirety of the Buddha-world in a single particle of dust. It is the single particle of dust which contains in itself that holy miracle and sublime secret and sacred being of the whole. The one wild flower, unnoticed by the wayside, opens out upon and is inseparable from, the entire universe.

When Master Chi-ch'en was asked what was meant by the "way upward" commonly spoken of in the Zen tradition, he responded by saying, "You will hit it by descending lower."[3] It is this ascent by means of descent, this discovery of the sublime in the commonplace, this revelation of the totality in the slightest particular, that is so characteristic of Zen. Surely the celebrated Chinese matter-of-factness and practicality is evident here, bringing a refreshing clearheadedness and directness and simplicity to the Mahayanist tradition. But just as surely the dimension of wonder and mystery is present as well, though in its own inverted, down-to-earth manner. As Suzuki insisted, "In spite of its matter-of-factness, there is an air of mystery and spirituality in Zen, which was later on developed into

90

a form of nature-mysticism. [Some] think Zen is the revolt of Chinese psychology against abstruse Buddhist metaphysics. But the fact is that it is not a revolt but a deep appreciation. Only the appreciation could not be expressed in any other way than in the Chinese way."[4]

The distinctiveness in this Chinese (and Zen) outlook lies in its peculiar combination of accepting the concrete "suchness" (*tathata*) of the mundane particular, while at the same time realizing the inexhaustible significance and mystery in the most commonplace object or situation. This is further reason why the comic spirit, which is so much at home in the this-worldly, and takes such delight in inversions and surprises, is so much at home in Zen, and why in Zen the relationship between mystery, comedy, and the earthy and every-day is so clearly articulated.

The master clown Grock in his autobiography, *Life's a Lark*, saw the special genius of his occupation as that of "transforming the little, everyday annoyances, not only overcoming, but actually *transforming* them into something strange and terrific." It is "the power to extract mirth for millions out of nothing and less than nothing: a wig, a stick of grease paint, a child's fiddle, a chair without a seat."[5] This is also a part of the special genius of Zen, the difference being that such a transformation-power presupposes that there is already something strange and terrific about the little everyday objects and trifling events which is usually missed because of their familiarity or their apparent triviality. One looks for a miracle in the fantastic transformations of the Bodhisattva, when it is right there in the speck of dust, or the child's toy. When Chen-chi first became abbot, he was asked by a resident monk, "I hear that when Sakyamuni began his public life, golden lotus sprang from the earth. Today, at the inauguration of Your Reverence, what auspicious sign may we expect?" The new abbot replied, "I have just swept away the snow before the gate!"[6] Master Ch'ung-hui, when asked, "What is the Way?" replied, "White clouds cover the range of peaks, and hummingbirds hover on garden flowers."[7] Or one may cite Yun-men who, on picking up a piece of firewood which his monks had just gathered, tossed it on the ground before them with the remark: "The whole *Tripitaka* expounds only this thing!"[8]

It is this perception of the uncommon commonplaceness of things

91

that underlies much of the comic iconoclasm in Zen, and its collapsing of the categories of the sacred and the sublime. Again and again the point is stressed in Zen literature, art, and life. Ch'ang-ch'ing asked: "What is the language of the Tathagata [the Buddha]?" Pao-fu replied, "Come, have a cup of tea!"[9] Or Yun-men when asked to give some extraordinary statement for the enlightenment of his monks, replied in the most ordinary terms: "Pulling a plough in the morning, and carrying a rake home in the evening."[10] As Suzuki repeatedly maintained: "Wherever the spirit of Zen moves, everything that comes in touch with it acquires something of mystery about it. The oil jar carried by T'ou-tzu emits an ineffable glow; the ladle in the hand of Hsueh-feng is incalculably more than a wooden stick; the straw sandal on the head of Chao-chou is worth sharing a corner in the temple treasure house."[11]

In concert with this is the persistent Zen debunking of the religious search for the exotic and the supra-normal, as if this were the locus of the sacred and the true seat of Buddha and Dharma. The Japanese master, Bankei (1622-93), for instance, was once interrupted during a sermon by a zealous Shin-shu priest. "The founder of our sect," boasted the priest, "has such miraculous powers that he held a brush in his hand on one bank of the river, his attendant held up a paper on the other bank, and the teacher wrote the holy name of Amida through the air. Can you do such a wonderful thing?" Bankei replied simply, "Perhaps your fox can perform this trick; but that is not the manner of Zen. My miracle is that when I feel hungry I eat, and when I feel thirsty I drink."[12] A similar tale is told of Huang-po who, while walking with another monk, came to a river. As Huang-po stood wondering how to get across, the other monk walked across the river without even getting his feet wet. When Huang-po saw this he exclaimed, "Oh, I didn't know he could do this; otherwise I should have pushed him right down to the bottom of the river."[13]

The same emphasis is given in one of the more popular koans, which plays upon the legend of the wondrous visitations of Niu-t'ou that ceased after his Zen awakening: "How was it that before Niu-t'ou had met the Fourth Patriarch, the birds used to flock to him with flowers in their beaks, while after his enlightenment the prodigy ceased?"[14] Yun-men is characteristically far less circumspect about the matter. He once related the legend to his monks, according to which the Buddha at his birth pointed toward heaven with one hand and the earth with the other, and taking seven steps forward looked toward the four quarters of the earth, exclaiming: "Above and beneath heaven I alone am the Honoured One." Yun-men then declared: "If I had seen him at the time, I would have cut him down with my staff, and given his flesh to dogs to eat, so that peace could prevail over all the world."[15]

Many such Zen stories reflect the same suspicion and humorous skepticism of the goggling delight in the fabulous that is the perennial soil for the strange human fascination for wizards and magicians, ghosts and goblins, witches and demons. For in excess such fascination provides too great a diversion from the principal human tasks and dilemmas, if not a camouflage of the real issues at hand, as well as a devaluation of what then become, by contrast, the commonplaces of human experience. In this reaction lies a profound sense of the ambiguity of the sacred which, though it may be seen as that which gives meaning and worth to the profane sphere over against which it sets itself apart, yet at the same time it may by its very separateness and elevation tend to empty the profane sphere of significance and value. In the claim that this sacred reality is the infinite source and repository of all power and worth lies the apparent negation of the possibility for any intrinsic power and worth in things themselves. As a result, offering itself as the ultimate basis of salvation, it may instead either elicit a defiant emptying of the heavens and repudiation of all sacrality in favor of secularity, or become the place of evasion and retreat, a refuge from reality rather than a response to it.

In either case what is missed is the suchness and wondrousness of things in themselves, however commonplace and seemingly inconsequential. As one master exclaimed, "The beauty of a mountain is that it is so much like a mountain, and of water that is so much like water." This is the acceptance and celebration of things as they are: beyond and before all thought of useful and useless, subject and object, mine and not-mine, good and bad, holy and unholy, marvellous and ordinary. It is the suchness of the flower—even the lotus flower—which is not first of all a sign or symbol that stands for something else, and that points away from itself to some other, more important, more sacred and more desirable something. The flower is a flower. That is its meaning, its purpose, its goodness, and its mystery. The flower points primarily to its flowerness, indeed to the particular flowerness of that particular flower. A flower means a flower. What greater value and importance and holiness and miraculousness can it have than this? If its function is simply to point away from itself, or to be caught up in some other meaning, instead of its gaining in worth and significance, it is actually emptied of its own meaning and being in order to serve in this depreciating capacity of "meaning" something else. Instead of the Buddha holding up the lotus flower (or, in the case of the wordless sermon on Vulture Peak, the sandal-wood flower), the lotus flower must then hold up the Buddha.

It was Ch'ing-yuan who announced: "Before I underwent (Ch'an) training, I saw mountains as mountains, and rivers as rivers. After I had called on enlightened persons, I managed to enter (Ch'an) and saw mountains were not mountains, and rivers were not rivers. Now that I have stopped (my false discriminating thought), I see that mountains are mountains and rivers are rivers, as before."[16] Nan-chu'an's answer to the question, "What is the Tao?" is most revealing of the Zen mind in this. "Your everyday mind is the Tao." Here "everyday mind" (p'ing-ch'ang hsin) points to nothing esoteric or supernatural or abnormal, no fantastic psychic state or ecstatic trance, nor any exalted gnosis available only to some inner circle of privileged elite. It is of course the everyday mind seen in a different light, the uncommon light of *satori*. But Zen does not dwell in the ivory tower of uncanny religious experience; it lives in the world of the everyday. Therefore, though in relation to the unenlightened it may be an extraordinary way of perceiving things, from the Zen standpoint it is perfectly ordinary; for it is perceiving things in a completely natural way through one's "original mind."

This relationship between suchness, mystery, and the comic-mundane was most simply, yet profoundly, expressed in the exclamation of P'ang Chu-shih:

> How wondrous this, how mysterious!
> I carry fuel, I draw water.[17]

The immediate inclination in interpreting these lines is to see in them a very serious and sobering realization of the awesome mystery that interpenetrates even the most menial activity, such as carrying fuel and drawing water, and a startling awareness of the "isness" of things, quite apart from judgments of meaning, value, and utility. This is certainly there. Yet something else is there, too; and that is the comic perception of suchness and mystery, the response of laughter to the sudden discernment of the most commonplace things in a new light, the surprised amazement over the wondrousness of the simplest task and the humblest of elements.

Once when all the monks attached to Master Tai-chu were engaged in tilling their farm, there was one monk who, upon hearing the dinner drum, at once raised his spade and gave out a hearty laugh and went off. Tai-chu remarked: "What an intelligent fellow! This is the way to enter the Kuan-yin gate of truth." When he returned to the monastery, he sent for the monk and inquired, "What was the truth you saw awhile ago when you heard the drum?" Answered the monk, "Nothing much, master. As I heard the dinner drum go, I went back and had my meal." This time it was the master who gave out a hearty laugh.[18] This immediate intuition of the sacred suchness of even so profane a matter as dinner and its summons has itself a comic dimension, and is often accompanied by laughter. For laughter, too, is a "breaking through the intellectual barrier; at the moment of laughing something is understood; it needs no proof of itself."[19] The moment of insight, which abruptly perceives with unshrouded clarity things-in-themselves, and at the same time with equal clarity the wondrousness of their inscrutable mystery, is marked as appropriately by laughter as by hushed reverence. Indeed such laughter is itself a form of reverence; it is the laughter of acceptance, appreciation, and wonder.

This is made explicit in Tsu-yuan's description of the moment and occasion of his enlightenment: "Looking up to the sky I laughed loudly, 'Oh, how great is the Dharmakaya [the most exalted of the three 'bodies' of the Buddha, hence the fundamental level of reality]! Oh, how great and immense for evermore!' Thence my joy knew no bounds."[20] It is this moment, however trifling the occasion, toward which much of Zen attempts to lead, or give expression to, a moment in which the sublime and the ridiculous, the monumental and trivial,

95

seriousness and laughter, meet in an experience which contains them both in a joyful acceptance and celebration of existence.

The 20th-century Japanese master Taji lay on his death bed. His senior monks had gathered around him to pay their respects and receive any final words of wisdom which he might have for them. One of the monks, recalling the master's fondness for a certain cake, had brought him a piece from a Tokyo shop, which the master feebly tasted. The senior monk asked if Taji had any special word for them. "Yes," responded Taji weakly, "This cake is delicious."[21]

The Playfulness That Cannot Be Netted

Of related significance is the use of ambiguity and indefiniteness in Zen and Zen art. Ambiguity is a part of the province of comedy, made most explicit in the double-meanings of puns and plays upon words, but also in the rather amorphous habit of the clown and fool, their blurring of distinctions and conventional discriminations, and the unpredictability of their behavior. Reality cannot be pinned down, netted, boxed, or frozen. In this lies the perennial threat posed by the comic in relation to the sacred, to reason and order, to "clear and distinct ideas," to the crispness of all boundaries and delineations. For the comic jest or jester does not simply profane Beauty, Truth, Goodness and Holiness, but rather muddies them, places their purity and preciseness somewhat in doubt, and calls them to a vague, chartless no-man's land between competing categories and forces. This ambiguity itself heralds that "wondrous playfulness" that moves within all phenomena, disturbing all the labelled drawers of the mind, emptying them and sporting with their contents, returning both form and content to the inexhaustible source of their being.

In Zen painting the employment of ambiguity and indefiniteness is especially apparent in the combined focus upon the suchness (*tathata*) of the concrete image and the Emptiness (*sunyata*) that is in and beyond that image. On both counts Zen art insists on being imprecise and incomplete. This is in marked contrast with Indian art, which moves away from the concrete actuality in favor of the stylized purity of an ideal form, and which avoids empty space in favor of a "finished" composition or profusely sculptured facade. Similarly,

1 Han-shan and Shih-te YEN-HUI

2 Three Sages Laughing on Tiger Creek SOGA SHOHAKU

3 Pu-tai dancing LIANG-K'AI

4 Bodhidharma MATABEI

5 The Bullfrog Buddha TOBA-SOJO. *From the Animal Scroll Scenes (choju-giga)*

6 Meditating frog
        SENGAI

'If by practicing zazen
One becomes a
            Buddha . . .'

7 Hui-neng tearing up the sutras LIANG-K'AI

8   Tan-hsia burning the Buddha-image   SENGAI

9 Self-portrait HAKUIN

10 Entering the city with bliss-bestowing hands SHUBUN, *after K'uo-an's Tenth Cow-herding picture*

His thatched cottage gate is closed; and even the wisest know him not. No glimpses of his inner life are to be caught; for he goes on his own way without following the steps of the ancient sages. Carrying a gourd he goes out into the market; leaning against a staff he comes home. He is found in company with winebibbers and butchers. He and they are all converted into Buddhas.

Bare chested and barefooted, he comes out into the market place;
Daubed with mud and ashes, how broadly he smiles!
There is no need for the miraculous power of the gods;
For he touches, and lo! the dead trees are in full bloom!

K'UO-AN

in traditional Western art there often appears to be a horror of the Void, and consequently an anxious concern to fill every point in the canvas with something, if only background and coloration. It is as if, as in classical Western physics, nature is supposed to abhor a vacuum, or, as in Western philosophy and theology, Nothingness implies the threatening, nihilating, chaotic abyss: the bottomless pit over which created things are precariously suspended. But in Zen, as in Taoism and Buddhism generally, formlessness is seen in very positive, dynamic, creative terms, and emptiness is the most appropriate designation for the ultimate reality and basic truth of all things.

In Indian Buddhism, artistic representation is involved in the paradox of attempting to point toward this emptiness by means of fullness, the Void by means of the All. For in the Indian tradition, much as in the classical Western tradition, the infinity and incomprehensibility and holy mystery at the root of all things is best suggested by means of a seemingly endless multiplicity of figures and a riot of detail, a representation of infinity by what appears to be a literal infinity of forms, as reflected in both Indian art and architectural adornment. This tradition is continued in the richness and grandeur of the Mahayanist art and literature that invaded China. But in Zen art, and that of the Sung dynasty contemporaneous with its beginnings, these concerns are arrived at in an opposite way: intimations of infinity and transcendence, of sublimity and mystery, are achieved through a creative use of empty space and indefiniteness of form.

This Oriental perception of the profundity of empty space was most amenable to a suggestion of the Void, an emptiness which is not simply a blank space, or unfinished space, or waste space, and not simply nothing at all, but in its own way a powerful, mysterious, blissful nothingness, full of potentiality and life. It is not merely the absence of forms or of light, nor the negation of these, but the presence of all vitality, purity, simplicity, immensity. As Huang-po said of emptiness: "All these phenomena are intrinsically void, and yet this Mind with which they are identical is no mere nothingness. By this I mean that it does exist, but in a way too marvellous for us to comprehend. It is an existence which is no existence, a non-existence which is nevertheless existence. So this true Void does in some marvellous way 'exist'."[22]

The full employment of this occurs in Southern Sung (1126-1279) painting in conjunction with the movement away from solidity of representation to a more suggestive sketching of bare outlines and minimal features (the *p'o-mo* manner). By "emptying" the forms of solidity and elaborate detail, and by a creative use of empty space, the artist is simultaneously able to capture both the suchness of the object beneath all the superimposed categories of rationality, value and utility, and the inexhaustible mystery within the object, the mystery of the Void. The *ch'i* (spirit), therefore, that informs the composition throughout is that of grasping both the transparent suchness and the infinite elusiveness of things. It is an artistry that, by means of concrete but indefinite imagery, reveals the lucid yet unfathomable character of existence, and its inexpressibility except in ambiguously suggestive terms, which therefore both disclose and cloak its reality. As Lytton Strachey phrased it, in contrasting Greek and Chinese art and poetry: "Greek art is. . . the most finished in the world; it is forever seeking to express itself completely and finally. [Chinese art] aims at producing an impression which, so far from being final, must be merely the prelude to a long series of visions and of feelings. It hints at wonders; and the revelation it at last gives us is never a complete one; it is clothed in the indefinability of our subtlest thoughts."[23]

The poetic ideal of *yugen* (depth or mystery), developed in Japanese poetry in the 12th century, is similarly achieved by a certain imprecision or vague intimation in language and imagery, or by the ambiguity of the language itself, which offers a pool of meaning rather than a unilinear suggestion. This is also apparent in many of the later haikus which, on the one hand, are quite precise in their reference to the most everyday objects and events, and in their restriction to seventeen scrupulously chosen syllables. Yet at the same time they contain an utter simplicity and absolute minimum of expression that can only begin to hint in the direction of experiences which words-unending could never grasp or exhaust.

The same achievement is visible in the Noh plays, with their use of a plain stage, a modicum of props, obscure language, and symbolic gestures. They "don't come right out and say what they're after," as an unsympathetic tourist might well remark. It is not, however, just that something is left for the imagination, and consequently for the creativity and participation of the observer—the point customarily made of the matter—but that nothing, however simple and commonplace, can be completely imaged or contained or exhausted at the rational and phenomenal level. Art, therefore, like life, must conceal its point as much as it reveals it, as in the artful artlessness of the Tea Ceremony.

This is also, interestingly, at the very heart of comedy, which in an analogous manner relies upon the double meanings of words, gestures, and situations—their ambiguity—for triggering laughter. The comic spirit and perspective is thus particularly suited to effecting the kind of deeper realization of the inner nature of things which Zen and Zen art is after. As a result, the sudden perception of this element of ambiguity, and of the underlying suchness and mystery of things, even the most ordinary and trivial, is often expressed by laughter— as Blyth has termed it, "the laughter of surprised approval."[24] This is quaintly illustrated in the Zen tale of Yao-shan who had climbed the mountain near his monastery for a walk. When he saw the moon suddenly appear from behind the clouds, he laughed heartily, so much so that his laugh echoed for ninety *li* east of the monastery. In the morning the villagers inquired of one another as to who was laughing so raucously in the middle of the night, disturbing everyone's sleep. Finding that it was not the laughter of any of the villagers, they concluded (suggesting that Yao-shan had a reputation for this type of behavior): "Last night the master gave us the greatest laugh of his life at the top of the mountain."[25]

One of the functions of the comic is to call attention to the element of ambiguity in all things, an ambiguity which admits of different interpretations and perceptions, none of which should be absolutized or taken with absolute seriousness. Here comedy is a reminder of the finiteness and fallibility of all individual perspectives. Comedy also points to a further ambiguity, and that is the ambiguity in which the same concern can be treated as sacred and sublime and therefore serious, and yet comic and therefore humorous. As in the case of Yao-shan, the response of awe upon seeing the moon and the response of laughter are both appropriate responses, and both reveal something about the nature of reality. Both point in their own way to the dimension of suchness and mystery beyond the matter-of-fact level of perception (i.e., the mere noticing of the moon), and beyond the distorted seeing of the discriminating-mind. The sudden realization of this is as amusing as it is sobering, as filled with playfulness as with earnestness, even though the heavy-handedness and soberness of most religion tends to channel this realization in the latter direction. Is reality, after all, really serious, as we so habitually suppose, and not humorous? Is the ponderous movement of the planets, or the darting of little fishes, actually to be construed as a serious motion? And what of Kikaku's

> *Tree frog, clinging*
> *To a banana leaf,*
> *And swinging, swinging.*

Or what is one to do with Issa's

> *Giant firefly:*
> *That way, this way, that way, this—*
> *And it passes by.*[26]

Does not their being and doing lie beyond the distinction between seriousness and laughter, such that to approach them only seriously, and to see them only in their seriousness, is a distortion of the first order? Is this great drama not also as great a comedy? And is this sober work not also a marvellous form of play, a prodigious frolicking of whirling galaxies and whirling atoms and whirling whirligigs?

On the one hand it may be said that comedy, like beauty, is in the eye of the beholder, and therefore that seeing things in comic perspective is a matter of the way in which the world appears, rather than a quality intrinsic to things themselves. Yet to be satisfied with this subjectivist statement of the situation (and its separation of subject and object) is often to ignore the alternative presuppositions which may unconsciously substitute themselves—namely, that reality is fundamentally "serious" or "dramatic" or "at work." In this way the denial of any epistemological and ontological appropriateness to the images and metaphors related to the comic very easily becomes an unexamined confirmation of another set of basic images and metaphors. From the Zen standpoint, one must someway cut through, not only such onesidedness, but the distinction between sides, whether subjective versus objective, dramatic versus comic, or work versus play. Wu-men, for example, in a verse written upon his *satori*, captures in a higher unity all these dimensions:

> *From the blue sky, the sun glowing white—a peal of thunder!*
> *All living things on earth open their eyes widely;*
> *Multiplicities endless uniformly bow their heads in respect;*
> *Lo and behold, Mt. Sumeru is off its base folk-dancing merrily!*[27]

Absurdity in the Comic Mode

The twentieth century has been introduced to a sense of the absurd with a vengeance that is in no small measure the result of the failure of, and inevitable reaction to, an overweening effort to bring all things under the dominion of human reason, progress, and control. Consequently our experiences of irrationality, meaninglessness, and chaos are deeply tragic. Yet absurdity is also at the heart of comic awareness. It is the abrupt perception of absurdity that triggers laughter (the comic twist). Humor plays with nonsense and foolishness. Joking delights in the irrational. Clowns incarnate confusions and contradictions. And comedy, unlike drama or any serious literary structure, refuses to abide by the same requirement to make sense, to conform to a plot, or to uphold the canons of law and order. Each of these forms has, to be sure, a certain logic of its own. But it is a logic based upon absurdity, and employing almost every conceivable violation of the commonly accepted categories of rationality, value, purpose, goodness, beauty, and holiness. Yet in this comic perception of absurdity lies the potential for a deeper level of insight into the element of absurdity in all things, even the most obvious and assured, and for a deeper level of acceptance and celebration of things in spite of their final recalcitrance to human patterns and designs.

There is, of course, a laughter of cynicism and despair which shouts out some last gesture of futility in the darkness—an heroic, perhaps, but nevertheless bitter flourish in the face of the bankruptcy of foundering systems. Yet this is not the comic spirit, which also deals with absurdity but does so more freely. The comic spirit does

101

not come into being at the end of the rope, or upon the loss of all bearings, which would make of it a grimace, or a hollow guffaw. It is something far more positive and basic, buoyant, and overflowing with laughter. In fact, in large part, the tragedies and absurdities of our time—and the death of all but a grotesque laughter which they bring—are the consequence of a prior refusal to give due recognition and place to the comic spirit.

In the twentieth century the problem of absurdity has become particularly acute in the West—e.g., the existentialism of Sartre, the "theatre of the absurd" and the work of various playwrights from Chekhov to Ionesco, Robbe-Grillet, Beckett, and Albee. This is partly because of an anxious and increasingly desperate attempt within the history of Western theologies and ideologies to define a substratum of meaning, purpose, and destiny in life. With the shattering of so noble a presumption we are shocked, disillusioned, dismayed. This is also because of an all-pervasive seriousness about the attempt, and a failure to cultivate laughter in relation to the stubborn refusal of things to fit into the neat patterns of rationality and order devised for them. It is the failure to discover laughter, both in absurdity and the attempted overcoming of absurdity, and to perceive a dimension of playfulness, as it were, in all things which transcends the oppositions between meaning and meaninglessness, purpose and purposelessness, value and valuelessness.

It is the absence of this attempt, so characteristic of Western intellectual history, to press existence for reason and purpose—or conversely to despair over absurdity and the tragic absence of the good, the true, and the beautiful in everything—that has enabled the Chinese and Japanese generally to have a singular acceptance of life as it is, to see through to the suchness and mystery of things beyond the schemas of intellection and value judgment, beyond the towering hierarchies and grand systems, and to do so with grace and good humor. In this earthiness and its devotion to the simplest particulars of life—quite apart from any cumbersome intellectual structures which are supposed to give them a place and to guarantee their worth, but which unfortunately have the bad habit of suffering periodic collapses—lies that uncommon wisdom, that fine sense of the comic, that affirmation of things in themselves, which is crystallized in Zen.

There is, after all, an element of absurdity in even the most accepted truths and established facts and conventions, as in the experience of using a familiar word that suddenly looks or sounds funny, that suddenly is absurd, like all words. This is one of the things which comedy—and Zen—so well perceive. Even that which makes most sense, which is beyond doubt, which is knowledge common to us all, suddenly seems to make no sense at all, to defy rationality, to be completely dubious and ambiguous, and shrouded in profound mystery. As Santayana put it, "Existence. . .is comic inherently. . . This world is contingency and absurdity incarnate, the oddest of possibilities masquerading momentarily as fact."[28] On the one hand this is the suchness of things, a perception lying beyond their utility, their value, their mental classification, as well as their sense, purpose, and meaning. Things are seen perfectly clearly beyond the filter of categories and in an unusually fresh and lucid light. On the other hand this suchness of things is at the same time a perception of their inexhaustible mystery—not in the sense of the mystery story which will be solved on the final page of the detective's investigation, and therefore no longer constitute a mystery, but in the sense of an ultimate mystery that is to be found in even the most obvious and ordinary areas of experience where no particular problem appears at all, and where no absurdity is immediately apparent.

A contemporary Zen anecdote tells of a roshi who lay dying. His monks had all gathered around his bed, from the most senior to the most novice monk. The senior monk leaned over to ask the dying master if he had any final words of advice or instruction for his monks. The old master slowly opened his eyes and in a weak voice whispered, "Tell them Truth is like a river." The senior monk passed this bit of wisdom in turn to the monk next to him, and it circulated around the room. When the words reached the youngest monk he asked, "What does he mean, 'Truth is like a river'?" The question was passed back around the room to the senior monk who leaned over the bed and asked, "Master, what do you mean, 'Truth is like a river'?" Slowly the master opened his eyes and in a weak voice whispered, "OK, Truth is *not* like a river."

There are some immediate similarities between the humorous effect of this comic reversal and the logical method of Nagarjuna—

and significantly Nagarjuna is cited as one of the precursors of Zen in dharma-succession from the Buddha. Nagarjuna's method may be seen as an attempt to demonstrate the equivalence of alternative philosophical positions. They are both true and untrue. By countering and contradicting each other, alternative philosophical positions demonstrate the futility of trying to comprehend reality by means of an intellectual system. The intent is not to show that existence is absurd after the manner of the French existentialists, or cognitively meaningless after the manner of the logical positivists (e.g., A.J. Ayer). The intent, rather, is to point up the absurdity in trying to grasp after meaning and cling to reality by means of this or that philosophical system.

A monk who practiced under Ma-tsu was once asked to deliver a letter from his master to the National Teacher, Hui-chung. After delivering the letter, the monk was asked by the National Teacher what doctrine Ma-tsu was teaching his students. The monk answered, straightforwardly enough, "The human mind is the very Buddha." The National Teacher asked, "What kind of phrase is this? Apart from this, does Ma-tsu have any other teaching?" The monk replied, "Yes: there is no mind, no Buddha."[29]

If the use of the term "absurdity" is acceptable in Zen as representing the inadequacy and final frustration of reason, and of the nonsensical methods employed to effect a leap beyond intellection, it is not a category implying despair or alienation or anxiety as in Western existentialism. If anything, it is a perception of absurdity that precipitates laughter, not despair, and that moves beyond alienation and anxiety into a joyful wonder. It does not arise out of the loss of a sense of meaning in life. No great light has failed; no sacred vision has been lost or become impossible. Indeed enlightenment has occurred, and everything has been gained. It is not the dark abyss of infinite nothingness that has been entered, but that blissful, wondrous emptiness wherein lies all fullness. It is in no way anxious or estranged, or condemned to an alienated consciousness; but is free in that freedom where inner harmony and well-being are not fettered to the attempt at coercing and possessing the world, or turning it into a problem, or offering an academic solution.

Chief Minister Ts'ui once came to the master Ju-hui with the familiar Mahayanist question about the universality of the Buddha-nature. In this case he asked, cleverly, "Does a sparrow have Buddha-nature?" Ju-hui responded, "Yes, it has." "Then," asked the minister, "Why does it make droppings on the head of the Buddha?" Ju-hui replied, "Yes, and why does it not do it instead upon the head of a sparrow-hawk?"[30]

The Zen appreciation and employment of absurdity is also not to be confused with a retreat into a kind of impregnable sarcasm, nor with a surrender to a blind or exhausted acquiescence. Rather, as in the Japanese use of the term *sono-mama* ("just-so-ness"), it is a matter of "taking things as they are" in a fundamental act of acceptance and celebration of life, which is hardly reducible to conservatism or resignation, let alone a sneering contempt or satiric defiance. Its kindred spirit, in fact, is none other than humor, which has its own salutary way of appropriating absurdity and irrationality. As James Sully has suggested, "while satire, sarcasm and their kind seem to be trying to push things away, or at least to alter them, humor, curiously enough, looks as if it were tenderly holding to the very world which entertains it."[31] It is this tenderness that is evident in the haiku, or in Zen paintings such as Mu-chi's "Monkeys" and "Crane," or in P'ang Chu-shih's carrying fuel and drawing water, or Yuan-wu's particle of dust and solitary blossom.

What, after all, is the point or value to be assigned to the little wild flower—on the basis of which we might imagine ourselves capable of accepting and affirming and being grateful for its existence—the wild flower that, like the millions of generations that have preceded it, pushes its delicate face up to the sunlight filtering into the forest glade, and dares anyone to make sense out of it? Into what cosmic plan does one fit the millenia of dinosaurs, or the teeming life of the sea? Or what is the meaning of the butterfly that briefly climaxes a bizarre metamorphosis through several identities in a crazy zig-zag pattern of erratic flight? What is the sense in the meandering path of a mountain stream, or the sermon being given in the babbling nonsense of the brook? What is the purpose of the millions of galaxies and their billions of stars, or the use of the millions of common flies and their billions of eggs? And what of all the waste space in space—if not as a sign of the playfulness and sheer thereness (or not-thereness)

of things which stubbornly refuse to conform to our rational patterns
and designs, or to our egotistic presumption that all things must defer
to our moral and religious requirements?

> *The moor hens sing,*
> *And to their tempo—look!—the clouds*
> *Are hurrying.*

Issa[32]

Religion often deals with questions of meaning, purpose and
value, and precariously attempts to assign a significance and structure
to things. Yet at the same time it deals with that level of mystery,
and absurdity, which transcends all such categories. Though it may
expend considerable effort in defining and preserving, through
symbol, myth and ritual, certain elemental truths and virtues which
it feels itself compelled to uphold, still it falls far short of the *mysterium*
out of which it arises, and to which it points, if it does not also affirm
and celebrate the isness, the thereness, the sheer suchness of things,
and participate joyfully in existence even when it doesn't play according to the rules and expectations set up for it. In Van der Leeuw's
words: "The religious significance of things. . .is that one which no
wider or deeper meaning can follow. It is the meaning of the whole:
it is the last word. But this meaning is never understood, this last
word is never spoken; always they remain superior, the ultimate
meaning being a secret which reveals itself repeatedly, only nevertheless to remain eternally concealed. It implies an advance to the
farthest boundary, where only one sole fact is understood: that all
comprehension is 'beyond'."[33]

This appreciation of mystery, this delighted wonder, is not simply
the consequence of some abstract reflection upon things, and therefore
a rational dislocation that Zen is seeking to overcome. It is rather
the profoundest level of human experience in relation to which we
so often misguidedly entertain the rationalistic conceit of attempting
to define and confine and, in the process, ultimately overcome this
mystery. It stands as the limit, the boundary, the end of all thought.
As Suzuki has expressed it, "When a man faces this mystery one
day in his life, he is filled with the mystic sense which goes utterly
beyond intellection."[34] Here it is no longer a matter of a problem

106

to be solved, a puzzle to be put together, or a curiosity that will open its peculiarities to patient observation. No amount of philosophical reasoning or scientific investigation or religious inquiry can net it and capture it and add it, like another species of intellectual triumph, to the informational zoo of human knowledge. The common confusion between this ultimate sense of mystery and mystery in the sense of problem-solving is remarkably absent in Zen, especially because of its sensitivity to mystery in the most common-place, obvious, taken-for-granted—and therefore presumably well-known—areas of experience. Zen comes to terms with absurdity long before it becomes the traumatic problem, or reaches the crisis proportions, so familiar in Western philosophical and religious thought.

This fundamental experience of absurdity is not, however, a withdrawal into a sheer agnosticism which sees and knows nothing in relation to the mystery of the Void, and which in a sense of futility or despair, or in simple boredom or fatigue, turns away to more manageable concerns. Nor is it an absolutism in relation to which everything is now seen and known completely in some higher wisdom of omniscience. In Suzuki's phraseology again, "All things come out of an unknown abyss of mystery, and through every one of them we can have a peep into the abyss."[35] On the one hand this is an "unknown abyss of mystery" with respect to which the claim to know the infinite depths of this abyss is only the comedy of a new ignorance and pretension. On the other hand, inasmuch as all things are manifestations of this abyss, and ultimately one with it, "through every one of them we can have a peep into the abyss."

It is this understanding that is captured in the utter simplicity of Basho's haiku:

> *Coming along the mountain path*
> *I am somehow mysteriously moved*
> *By these violets.*[36]

Such a perception can be interpreted soberly as the experience of awe and wonder, of marvel and amazement, of sublimity, when confronted by even so fragile and insignificant a particular as a violet turning its tiny face up to the light. But soberness is not enough, nor does it reflect the whole of the experience. With equal legitimacy this perception can be interpreted comically as the sudden awareness of the absurdity, the nonsense, the pointless thereness of the flower which, tiny and helpless though it might be, defies all attempts at coercing it into conformity with the categories of rationality and value and purpose, at fitting it into a system, at "discovering" its utility, or at making it the object of desire, attachment, and possession. The mode of perception and experience toward which Zen points is really defined by both moments and both expressions. It is the combination of sublimity and absurdity, of reverence and humor, of amazement and laughter, that arises out of the transparent thusness, yet ineffable mystery of all being. It is a level of spiritual and aesthetic achievement which, as Huizinga said of poetry, "lies beyond seriousness, on that more primitive and original level where the child, the animal, the savage, and the seer belong, in the region of dream, enchantment, ecstasy, laughter."[37]

CHAPTER SEVEN

The Folly of the Desiring Self

*A monk once announced himself, giving his full name. Master
Tung-shan asked, "Which one is your real self?" The monk
replied, "The one who is standing before you." "What a pity!"
responded Tung-shan. "People of today are all like this. They
take the front of an ass, or the rear of a horse, and call it
themselves!"*

TRANSMISSION OF THE LAMP

Zen folly is the other side of human folly: the comic reflection of
ego, ignorance, desire, and attachment. Foolishness is sometimes best
overcome, not by a grand display of wisdom and sage spiritual
counsel, but by a higher foolishness—which is one of the reasons
religions need not only masters and seers, but clowns and fools, or
masters and seers who are both. The foolishness of the enlightened
is the wisdom for fools; and the impiety of the holy is the means of
salvation from the false piety of the unenlightened. In an apparent
madness the real madness of the desiring self is revealed; by seeming
ignorance the world of ignorance is mocked.

King of Monkeys

The comic folly of ego, ignorance, and desire is effectively
captured in the celebrated tale of the monkey king Sun Wu-kung, from
the Chinese classic *Journey to the West*, a legendary account of the
travels of the Buddhist pilgrim Hsuan-tsang to and from India in the
7th century. Sun Wu-kung, who needed to be tamed in order to
become a protector for the pilgrim on his treacherous journey, begins
the story as a rebellious upstart in the universe. Bored with his simple
life in the land of "fruits and flowers" and anxious to learn the secret
of immortality, Monkey left his Edenic paradise and travelled to India

109

to gain knowledge and power reputedly possessed by great yogis. There he obtained various yogic powers, including the power to transport himself great distances in an instant. Upon returning to China, and being proclaimed king of the monkeys, he gained further powers by stealing the secrets of metallurgy and weaponry from the Dragon of the Eastern Sea, and then the formula for immortality by eating the peaches in Peach Tree Garden, out of which the elixir of immortality was brewed.

Monkey proudly proclaimed himself "Great Sage, Equal of Heaven" and demanded his rightful place among the gods. He even proposed that he was more qualified to be king of the gods than the Jade Emperor. The gods were forced to respond and sent celestial troops to put down the rebel and his rebellion. A series of titanic battles ensued until finally, through the combined forces of Heaven, he was subdued and brought in chains to the heavenly court of the Jade Emperor. But before a trial could begin, Monkey broke free and raced around Heaven, smashing the furniture in the palaces of the gods and immortals. After he was subdued a second time an appeal was made to the Buddha to come and help deal with the situation.

When Monkey was brought before the Buddha, he defended himself by extolling his remarkable feats and the powers he had achieved, including the power to leap thousands of miles in a single bound. He was not repentant in the slightest, but repeated his demands to be named king of the gods, insisting that he was clearly superior to any of the gods. After listening patiently, the Buddha said, "You claim to possess all these powers. I'll wager that you cannot even jump over my hand." Monkey rose eagerly to the challenge: "How much do you want to bet?" The Buddha said, "The terms of the wager are that, if you do succeed in jumping over my hand, I will acknowledge that you are indeed 'Great Sage, Equal of Heaven,' and you will be given your rightful place among the gods. But if you cannot jump over my hand, you will have to return to earth and do penance for the rest of your life."

Monkey thought to himself, "the Buddha is the biggest fool I have ever met," and readily accepted the wager. He then proceeded to leap the greatest leap of his life. He even surprised himself. He leaped so far that he reached the outer edge of the universe. There he found five pillars, on which he wrote triumphantly, "Monkey, Great Sage, Equal of Heaven, was here." In a final gesture of defiance—and territorial claim—he urinated on one of the pillars. Then he leaped back to where the Buddha was waiting, confidently seeking his prize and acclamation. The Buddha thereupon held up his hand, on the five fingers of which were written, "Monkey, Great Sage, Equal of Heaven was here." A yellow stain streaked the index finger! The joke was on Sun Wu-kung, and he was forced to return to earth and do penance. To ensure his restraint, the Buddha had him placed in a secure cage, pinned down by five Chinese mountains. After 500 years he was released, with the probationary promise that he would use his powers for the protection of the Buddhist pilgrim to and from India!

The Comedy of Ego and Desire

Fools and their folly are commonly the subjects of comedy, particularly fools who are blissfully unaware of their folly, or fools who mistake their folly for wisdom. This, in Zen, describes the self-portrait of humanity. Humor, therefore, is not only a permissible, but an especially appropriate, way of getting at what in Buddhism has consistently been identified as the fundamental folly of the desiring self. The Sixth Patriarch was once approached by a young monk who had a rather proud air about him, which Hui-neng detected in his minimal bowing. Hui-neng asked the monk what he had to be proud about. The monk replied, "I have already recited the *Saddharma Pundarika Sutra* three thousand times." Hui-neng suggested, "If you understood the meaning of what you recite, you would not think it such a grand thing even if it had been recited ten thousand times."[2]

If the ego is seen as one of the elements of the human problem, then humor corresponds to the realization of the comedy of the substantial ego, the refusal to take the ego seriously or absolutely in its pretension of being the one secure point of reference in consciousness—as in the philosophy of Descartes where, when all else is in doubt, one retreats to the seemingly impregnable refuge of the reflective self: *cogito ergo sum.* There is no small irony in the fact that what is the fundamental illusion for Buddhist experience is taken

111

as the fundamental axiom of Cartesian thought. In Zen, especially, it is through humor that the ego is revealed as only the mask that the actor puts on, or holds in front of his face (as in the *Noh* play, or ancient Greek drama, or the original meaning of the Latin *persona* as "mask"), hiding his true identity, a mask which is both a tragic mask from the standpoint of ignorance and suffering, and a comic mask from the standpoint of enlightenment and liberation.

One is reminded in this of the bauble carried by many jesters in medieval and renaissance Christendom, with a carved representation serving as the head of the bauble-stick of themselves in their official identity and social role as fools. Common practice was to engage, in this fashion, in an extended conversation or debate with one's "self." The ego, as it were, was conveniently placed by the fool on the end of the stick for purposes of discussion, argument and disputation, or simply for hitting other people over the head![3] That, in Zen terms, is the meaning of ego. It is the mask which the fool wears, or ties to the end of his stick, but which has a way of gaining an autonomy and objective reality of its own, so much so that the fool (as a fool) comes to identify with it, and even to enter into the prolonged debate of the divided self. Such problems the fool has a special talent for exposing, either unawares or by design.

An incident is recorded in the *Transmission of the Lamp* in which Master Hui-chung was invited to the imperial palace for an audience with the Emperor. When Hui-chung did not look attentively at his Majesty, the irritated Emperor demanded to know "For what reason do you not look at the Emperor of the great T'ang Empire?" Hui-chung asked in turn, "Does Your Majesty look at the sky?" The Emperor replied, "Yes, we have looked at the sky." Hui-chung then asked, "Your Majesty, does it ever wink at you?"[4]

A similar point is made in the story of Keichu, a Zen master of the Meiji period. The Governor of Kyoto paid Keichu the honor of a visit. His presence was announced to the Zen master by an attendant who presented the Governor's calling card, which read: "Kitagaki, Governor of Kyoto." "I have no business with such a fellow!" snapped Keichu to the attendant, refusing to see him. "Tell him to get out of here!" When this was communicated to the Governor, instead of becoming incensed, he took a pen and scratched out the words, "Governor of Kyoto," and gave the card back to the attendant. When Keichu saw the card, he exclaimed, "Oh, is that Kitagaki? I wish to see him!"[5]

The 15th-century master Ikkyu was once invited to a banquet hosted by wealthy patrons of his temple. He came dressed in beggar's garb, and was summarily sent away by his hosts who did not recognize him. Ikkyu went back to his chambers and put on his purple ceremonial robe. When he reappeared at the banquet he was graciously welcomed. Upon entering he took off his purple robe, revealing the beggar's robe underneath. "Apparently," said Ikkyu, "you did not invite me, but the purple robe!"[6]

Through foolishness and humor, generally, the identities and distinctions to which we commonly give the utmost importance, and upon which we bestow the utmost seriousness and sacrality, are broken down. The rigidity and oppressiveness of the delineations of self and other, important and unimportant, good and bad, holy and unholy, great and small, are dissolved. And to the extent that this is so we are freed to laugh at ourselves and at the significance which we attach to ourselves, our roles, our boundaries, and our protective fences. The possibility is opened for us to hear, in Charles Morris' words,

> *The selfless laughter*
> *that can Buddha after Buddha*
> *spawn. . .*[7]

The Folly of the Desiring Self

Here, as Suzuki says of his *satori*, "my individuality, which I found rigidly held together and definitely kept separate from other individual existences, becomes loosened somehow from its tightening grip and melts away into something indescribable, something which is of quite a different order from what I am accustomed to."[8] Similarly, Kosen Imakita says of his awakening: "There was no before and after. Everything was as though suspended. The object of my own meditation and my own self had disappeared. The only thing I felt was that my own inner-most self was completely united and filled with everything above and below and all around."[9] Yun-men put it quite differently: when asked by a monk what Niu-t'ou was like after he

113

had seen the Fourth Patriarch, and been enlightened, he replied, "A cricket swallowing a tiger in a fire."[10] That is, the small "self" had been opened out to the infinite "Self which is no-Self" through the burning up of ego and its pretensions and self-deceptions. In the new and larger perspective that such an awakening brings, one penetrates Wei Wu Wei's "open secret" that "'self' and 'other' are the oldest and most ubiquitous pair of clowns—the very archetypes of all clowns and of all clownishness."[11]

An enlightenment experience is not, however, a guarantee that one has solved all problems or conquered all traces of ego. By no means. It is a beginning, not a conclusion. In fact, ego may simply reappear in new attire and with renewed force, wearing the halo and robe of self-righteousness. The great Rinzai master Hakuin confesses in his *Orategama* that, following his first satori at the age of twenty-four, his sense of elation soon turned into self-congratulation. "My pride soared up like a majestic mountain; my arrogance surged forward like the tide. Smugly I thought to myself: 'In the past two or three hundred years no one could have accomplished such a marvelous breakthrough as this.'" Confident in his attainment he then sought out his master Shoju to tell of his glorious enlightenment. Shoju was not as impressed and, after testing him with a koan, twisted Hakuin's nose and said to him: "You poor hole-dwelling devil! Do you think somehow that you have sufficient understanding?" After this incident Hakuin reports that "almost every time he saw me, the Master called me a 'poor hole-dwelling devil'."[12]

Similarly, if one takes the Buddhist emphasis upon the problematic of desire, there is something not only pathetic but comic about passion, greed, envy, jealousy, pride, and hatred. One is fully liberated in seeing both its pathetic and its comic side, both the suffering and the folly of insatiable grasping and inordinate profession. Thus an aspect of the experience of enlightenment in Zen may be seen as the realization of the forms of one's ignorance as foolish, so that a part of what the liberation of an awakening may mean is the freedom to laugh at the comedy of one's blindness, and to laugh in the joy of newfound insight. Tragic folly is also comic folly and not simply and oppressively tragic. Ignorance is blind, yet also blissfully stupid and bungling. The figure of the man of ego and passion, like that of the dog chasing its tail, is simultaneously pitiful and funny. For this reason the clown and fool, as the laughable personifications of nonsense and folly, can serve in their own buffoonish way as agents of awakening and illumination. They are the crooked fingers pointing to the moon.

The image of the fool is a common one in Buddhist teaching, as exemplified in the frequency of the term in the *Dhammapada*. It is the unwitting self-portrait of humanity; and the clown-fool is offered as the mirror in which we can see our reflection.

> *"These sons belong to me, and this wealth belongs to me,"*
> *With such thoughts a fool is tormented.*
> *He himself does not belong to himself;*
> *How much less sons and wealth?*
> *The fool who knows his foolishness is wise at least so far.*
> *But a fool who thinks himself wise,*
> *He is called a fool indeed...*
> *Fools of little understanding are their own greatest enemies,*
> *For they do evil deeds which must bear bitter fruit.*[13]

Likewise in Zen a part of the folly of the self desiring to make conquest of the non-self is that the result is the opposite of the intention: the possessor becomes the possessed. The desire to achieve dominion over persons and things is involved in a comic/pathetic reversal in which persons and things gain dominion over the self. At best it becomes increasingly unclear whether "the dog is wagging the tail or the tail is wagging the dog." As in so much of comedy, in the proud moment of achievement everything is suddenly inverted, and the victor becomes the victim—though the humor in the inversion is only appreciated when the process is halted.

The teaching of Chuang-tzu is also that of Zen:

> *When he tries to extend his power over objects,*
> *Those objects gain control over him.*
> *He who is controlled by objects*
> *Loses possession of his inner self.*[14]

In Zen this applies equally to the intellectual attempt at grasping reality, at knowing in the sense of capturing and mastering things. Hence, a significant part of Zen iconoclasm is involved in the smashing of rational categories and value structures, the moral judgements and mental discriminations according to significance and utility which we interpose between ourselves and the world of our perception. For the true reality is hidden behind the boxes and badges of relative value, goodness, and usefulness that serve instead to enmesh ourselves, as in a great net with which we have thought to trap reality, but have instead been trapped by our own devices. A monk once asked Ts'ao-shan, the co-founder of the Ts'ao-tung (Soto) sect: "What is the most prized thing in the world?" Ts'ao-shan responded: "A dead cat!" The monk asked, "Why is it so prized?" The master replied, "Because no one thinks of its value."[15]

There is something about this perspective, as in the comic perspective generally, that objects to the fixed, the definable, the formulated, whether it be legal, moral, social, or intellectual. It does so not only because it senses this as stifling the human spirit, but because it sees this as having an element of arbitrariness and illusion about it. In principle, therefore, it insists on the reality behind the facade, on the truth that resists final definition and formulation, or the outcome that baffles all canons of predictability. It defies every attempt at putting existence under the lock and key of rational law, moral convention, social structure, or considerations of worth or utility. Its adversaries are artificiality, consistency, and distinction, which it persistently thwarts with the surprises of arbitrariness, absurdity, and inversions of value. In so doing it points to a state in which none of the categories through which the world is divided up and supposedly conquered exist; for categories are the weapons of discrimination and possession. Here, too, "he that takes up the sword shall die by the sword."

Comic Distance and the Bonds of Seriousness

Often this realization of the folly of the desiring self is viewed only in terms of the dramatic mode to the exclusion of the comic. It is a "serious matter" and not a "laughing matter," in relation to which anything but the utmost gravity and solemnity seems inappropriate. Especially is this so inasmuch as the realization involved occurs in a religious context where, presumably, we understand ourselves to be dealing with issues of "ultimate concern" that seem, if anything,

to demand the ultimate in seriousness. The comic side of this realization, and the importance of humor and laughter in relation to it,
therefore, is commonly brushed aside as peripherally, or just accidentally, related to the difficulty and its resolution, if not a part of
the problem itself. The warnings of the German philosopher George
Friedrich Meier are representative of the misgivings of more than
German philosophers: "We are never to jest on or with things which,
on account of their importance and weight, claim our utmost
seriousness. There are things. . .so great and important in themselves,
as never to be thought of and mentioned but with much sedateness
and solemnity. Laughter on such occasions is criminal and indecent.
. .For instance, all jests on religion, philosophy, and the like important
subjects."[16]

But from the standpoint of both Zen and the comic spirit,
seriousness itself, however noble its motivations and commendable
its intentions, is also a sign of attachment and bondage. Seriousness
is a part of the same entanglements which seriousness would attempt
to overcome. For implicit in all seriousness is the inclination to take
one's self and one's situation *too* seriously. The fundamental problem
of ego, ignorance, and desire is, in a sense, precisely that of overcoming such seriousness. We fall, as it were, when we begin to take
ourselves and our separate identities, our desires and acquisitions,
our circumstances and fortunes, with the seriousness of those who
are the self-appointed centers of all things. In what we consider to
be an expression of our freedom, we lose our freedom by placing
ourselves in subservience to the demands of ego and desire, and under
the beck and call of anything that surrounds and affects us. Lin-chi's
characterization of the result is most accurate: "Look at the figure
in the puppet show, whose movements by another are controlled."[17]

Those with a keen sense of humor with respect to themselves,
their concerns, and convictions are to that extent free spirits. They
have achieved a comic distance which has refused that attachment
to self and things that spells bondage. They have not pinned their
happiness and well-being to the conditions of their lives or the consequences of their actions. In the objectivity of a comic detachment they
are not easily disturbed or threatened or conquered; for they have
learned to laugh at the folly of the desiring self, its grand schemes,

and its ensnaring involvements. This "detached involvement" of humor which refuses to absolutize, and thus to endow with absolute seriousness, anyone or anything, is to this extent, at least, a corollary of the Zen emphasis upon non-attachment, and in its Zen form a part of what that non-attachment means. Hui-neng asks, "What is Unconsciousness [*wu-nien*, or no-thoughtness, taking no thought]? It is to see all things as they are and not to become attached to anything; it is to be present in all places and yet not to become attached anywhere; it is to remain forever in the purity of self-nature; it is to let the six sense-robbers run out of the six sense-gates into the world of the six sense-objects, and yet not to become defiled therein, nor to get away therefrom; it is but to retain perfect freedom in going and coming."[18]

On the one hand it is important to be serious, concerned, committed, and involved; and these are praiseworthy virtues. On the other hand this in itself can become a new form of bondage, no matter how lofty its objective or how sincere its motivation. One should not even be too serious about Zen! The words of Ikkyu's *doka* are the comic parenthesis within which the zealousness of all efforts at conquering the self and saving the world must be seen:

> *Though we do not preach the doctrine,*
> *Unasked the flowers bloom in spring;*
> *They fall and scatter,*
> *They turn to dust.*[19]

One of the things the comic spirit and perspective achieves is a capacity to be serious, yet not in such a way as to take oneself or one's aspirations too seriously; to be earnest, but not caught up within earnestness; to be actively involved, while not determined by this involvement nor attached to the outcome of one's action; to be sincere, but not imprisoned in one's sincerity; to live intensely, yet not tensely or in tension. Such an achievement makes possible a living in the world without being conformed to it or bound by it. As Yun-men phrased it, "He speaks of fire without his mouth being burned by it."[20]

As long as one is completely immersed in and therefore circumscribed, defined, and determined by the little drama of the self and its situations, everything is quite sober and serious. A hushed mood of gravity and solemnity prevails. Trespassers on this holy ground must be punished or beaten off. The comic perception on the other hand is itself an emancipation, however momentary, from the fanaticisms of the ego and the tyranny of the situation. One has entered that freedom of spirit and liberty of detachment which opens up through seeing "self" and "situation" in a larger perspective. One has gone beyond seriousness and sobriety. As Suzuki comments in defense of the unusual comic emphasis in the poetry and art of the Japanese master, Sengai: "An event becomes humorous when it is taken out of its limited frame and placed in a larger one."[21] In humor there is transcendence and freedom. The free person is the one who is free to laugh, and to see things in the light of laughter. One is no longer in bondage to seriousness. What has been called the achievement of a "cosmic consciousness" in the transcendence of narrow, self-centered concerns is therefore also a "comic" consciousness. As Hermann Hesse writes in *Steppenwolf*: "Seriousness is an accident of time. It consists in putting too high a value on time. In eternity there is no time. Eternity is a mere moment, just long enough for a joke."[22]

Comic Heroism

The Zen roots of this perspective, on their Taoist side, go back to Chuang-tzu. When he was nearing death, his disciples wished to honor him with an elaborate funeral, but Chuang-tzu wanted nothing special. "The sky and earth will be my casket. I will be wreathed by sun, moon, and stars, and attended on every side by the ten thousand things. What finer preparations than these?" Then, to his disciples' concern that his body should not be exposed to the birds, Chuang-tzu responded, "Unburied I will be eaten by crows and vultures; buried I will be food for worms and ants. Why rob one to feed the other?"[23]

One of the special features of this attitude and spirit is its invulnerability. As Kuei-shan said of Po-chang, "He is an iron bull on whom mosquitoes may settle but can find no place to sting."[24] By not endowing one's person or cause or situation with an unqualified gravity, one has not been placed in the extremely vulnerable position of pinning all happiness and well-being to the precarious circumstances

119

and fortunes of one's existence. Otherwise, however grand the aspiration, however salutory the project, however commendable the ambition, the result is the same: one is inextricably tied to the result and its preservation. Seriousness, unmitigated, is itself a form of anxiety and craving, a restless clinging to self and grasping after the objects of its attachment. The posture and demeanor is that of one who is basically insecure and threatened, who has something to gain and therefore something to lose, who is afraid. The ultra-serious person lives essentially outside the self-nature, subservient to the beck and call of stimulus and response, like a reed tossed to and fro by every wind that blows. Such a person is never free to laugh in the self-contained laughter of inwardness.

The distinct impression, on the other hand, of the comic spirit and perspective in Zen is its invincibility—like the invincibility that has often been noticed in the person of the clown or fool. The comic figure cannot finally be conquered, defeated, or killed; for the Achilles' heel of ego, attachment, and desire is not there. Life is not lived in the closed circle of seriousness, but outside the common play of forces, like the clown or fool who stands outside the laws of society, of reason, and of anticipated appearance and behavior. What for the ordinary person would be fatal—to ego, pride, status, or self-image— the clown-fool accepts or shakes off with a resiliency that suggests access to some other plane of being. Like the comic characters in film cartoons who may be cut in shreds, smashed flat, riddled with holes, or stretched into a thin line, yet which suddenly spring back into their original form or are miraculously put back together, the clown always seems to survive. There is, as it were, no tree on which such a person can be hanged—as in the medieval legend of the court-fool Marcolf, who so enraged King Solomon that he ordered his guards to lynch Marcolf, with the sole concession being that the victim might select the hanging-tree. "So Marcolf and the servants travelled through the valley of Josaffat, and over the hill of Olivet, and from thence to Jericho, and over the river Jordan, and through all Arabia, and over the Grand Desert to the Red Sea, but they never found the tree on which Marcolf chose to be hanged!"[25]

The tragic hero dies, in a blaze of glory and a final shout of defiance perhaps; but the comic hero lives on, and in so doing is therefore the unexpected, incredible, and yet very real symbol of freedom, wisdom, life, eternity. If tragic heroes, whose ego and pride and whose duty and world are intensely serious matters, belong to death and winter, comic heroes belong, as Northrop Frye suggests, to spring and light and life.[26] In their own peculiar way they are the children of eternity and the agents of salvation. In their innocence and ignorance, their nonsense and foolishness, their apparent absurdity, they draw upon some larger wisdom. The chaos which happens to them, or which they bring about, is not death but new life, not darkness but light. It is the dissolution of the old order, the order of ego, desire and attachment, and the dawn of a new awakening and freedom. This is the other side of the double-image which the comic figure represents: not the archetype of folly and disorder, but the archetype of a new order and higher wisdom.

The tragic impulse is to separate things out from one another, carefully discriminating between categories of persons and things, both hierarchically and in terms of opposites. The tragic mentality is not only discriminatory and dualistic, but radically dualistic, to the point of dividing reality into competing and irreconcilable forces. Thus out of the history of tragedy (both in the theater and real life) comes the tragic collision, the *agon* as the Greeks called it, between pro*tagon*ists and an*tagon*ists. Combatants are pitted against each other, with both sides dedicated to a stubborn and unyielding defense of their principles, if need be to the last soldier, unwilling to seek compromise and accommodation.

Comedies, on the other hand, tend toward inclusiveness rather than exclusiveness, the both/and rather than the either/or, and thus to reconciliation rather than a rigid and militant polarization. Shakespeare's tragedies, for example, end invariably in destruction and death as forces in collision produce a vicious cycle of mutual annihilation. Shakespeare's comedies, on the other hand, end with parties reconciled, marriages, feasts, and celebrations. Hence the familiar dictum that tragedies end in funerals, while comedies end in weddings.

In these terms Zen may be said to be fundamentally comic. The Zen uses of humor, and the Zen spirit and perspective generally, share in the comic inclination to move toward reducing tensions, overcoming

121

conflicts, and including opposites in some larger unity. In so doing Zen reflects both the traditional Indian Buddhist critique of dualism and the Chinese vision of a harmony of opposites, as in the complementarity of the yang/yin cosmology.

Beyond Striving and Seeking

In this necessity of going beyond tragic seriousness, a Zen parody of Zen may be seen to be as important as an iconoclasm directed at the crassest forms of folly. When Ma-tsu said that "slippery is the slope of Shih-t'ou," this was not meant as a criticism, but rather as a compliment to Shih-t'ou's skill in preventing any attachment to form, person, idea or scheme, any resting-place outside of the self-nature. Anything can become the object of desire, attachment and therefore bondage, including, as Hui-neng insisted, desire even for purity of mind, or attachment to certain forms of meditation, which may only eventuate in another order of grasping and clinging. Hence his insistence upon sudden rather than gradual enlightenment; for true awakening and liberation must be that which flows forth naturally and spontaneously, and with an immediacy that precludes the distinction between what is sought for and the act of seeking for it. As long as one is in the process of seeking, one is unaware of the Buddha-nature that is prevenient to seeking, and the precondition of it. Hence the act of seeking and striving must itself be turned into the non-act of not-seeking and not-striving. Action as such in this context involves the very sources of ignorance and bondage from which one seeks to be free: ignorance of the Buddha-nature within, desire for realizing the Buddha-nature, dependence upon the means of realization, and attachment to means and ends. As Chuang-tzu, long before the emergence of Zen in China, had written:

> *Joy does all things without concern;*
> *For emptiness, stillness, tranquillity, tastelessness,*
> *Silence, and non-action*
> *Are the root of all things.* [27]

In Japanese Zen there are, of course, important differences between the Rinzai and Soto methods of cultivating *wu-wei* (not seeking or striving). Rinzai Zen, in a sense, encourages seeking and striving through the use of the koan method, in which one meditates on the koan problem, and is required to offer a spontaneous answer to the master in periodic and often traumatic *sanzen* sessions. But insofar as this encourages seeking and striving, it is in order to negate it by building up frustration and doubt to the point where all attempts to defend the ego and achieve a rational understanding are thwarted, and one is left with no alternative but to speak and act immediately and effortlessly out of one's "original nature." Thus, while from one standpoint the utmost seriousness and concerted effort may be required if one is to experience the freedom of enlightenment, from a larger standpoint such is not in itself the direct product of this seriousness and effort, in fact is not a product at all, but happens when one finally gives up, lets go, dies to self and desire, and exhausts all resources. It comes as if out of nowhere, as if miraculously by some special intervening act of grace. There must be a leap in the process, a break in the chain, analogous to, though not identical with, Kierkegaard's "leap of faith" and "suspension over twenty thousand fathoms."

In Hakuin's words, "If you want to get at the unadulterated truth of egolessness, you must once and for all let go your hold and fall over the precipice."[28] This leap into the abyss of emptiness in Zen is the "snapping of the bonds of ignorance," which is essentially an inward event, a manifestation of the self-nature, though commonly prompted by some outward event, as in the case of Hsiang-yen's enlightenment on hearing the ping of the tile he had thrown striking a stalk of bamboo. The external event, however, stands in an accidental and seemingly absurd relationship to the internal releasing of consciousness, and the process that precedes it. Precisely what event it is becomes a miscellaneous datum. It functions as an occasion for the truth to manifest itself, but is not a part of that truth.

Soto Zen, on the other hand, in down-playing the koan method and what appears to be the projected goal of having an experience of "being enlightened," argues that if one's original nature is Buddha, then one is already within enlightenment, and there can therefore be no path to enlightenment at all. This would be like Po-chang's "riding the ox in search of the ox." The way of Zen is therefore no way, if by this one means a journey to some foreign destination. It is a way only in the sense of working out, or manifesting, or expressing, the fundamental character of one's being. Hence, as Dogen (1200-53), the founder of Japanese Soto, insisted, one should "just sit" in zazen, for there is nowhere to go and nothing to achieve. There is no distant mountain to conquer, no spiritual ladder to climb, no river to cross. One is there in one's self-nature from the beginning.

In this apparent conflict one recognizes something of William James' classic distinction between the psychology of the *twice-born* and the *once-born*.[29] The Rinzai approach fosters the transformation of a consciousness that is seen as ensnared by illusions from which the individual must be released, and rescued from the false trails out of which the mind must be redirected. The Soto approach fosters a nurturing of a consciousness seen as fundamentally whole and pure, and needing only certain vehicles, like zazen, through which to manifest itself. The Rinzai method, as Christmas Humphreys suggests, "like the explosives used in logging, is designed to break the jam in the river, and let the waters and all which float thereon ride free."[30] The Soto attitude, in Alan Watts' imagery, is that "muddy water is best cleared by leaving it alone."[31] Originally, at least, these approaches must have addressed themselves to two different human conditions, though later they tended to become a matter of orthopraxy rather than a means of adjusting to individual differences.

Whichever the technique, however, both schools recognize that at a certain point (either from the beginning in "just sitting" or through some dramatic change) the goal must become a non-goal, seeking must turn into non-seeking, action into non-action. As Bodhidharma is reputed to have said, "All the attainments of the Buddhas are really non-attainments."[32] Or as Hui-neng preached, "When there is no abiding of thought anywhere on anything—this is being unbound. This not abiding anywhere is the root of our life."[33] Similarly, the *Vajracchedika* had defined non-attachment and non-striving as "letting thought arise without fixing itself anywhere."[34] In the moment of giving up the object of one's thought and desire and hoped-for possession is the moment of realization.

On this point both Lin-chi (Rinzai) and Dogen are in accord. Dogen insists that the monk should be purposeless: "Do not think about how to become a Buddha."[35] Lin-chi, likewise, characterizes the Zen person as one who has "not a thought of running after Buddhahood. He is free from such pinings. Why is it so with him? Says an ancient sage, 'When the Buddha is sought after, he is the cause of transmigration'."[36] Therefore Lin-chi maintains that a true seeker does not seek. "He simply walks when he wants to walk, and sits when he wants to sit, without a single thought of seeking Buddhahood. . .Do not follow others who are busying themselves aimlessly with their studies of Ch'an and Tao, their learning of names and sayings, and their quest of Buddha, Patriarchs, and enlightened masters. . .If your searching minds really come to an end, there will be no more anxiety for anything."[37] Hence the radical iconoclasm of Lin-chi's dictum that "Bodhi (enlightenment) and Nirvana are a stake to which donkeys are fastened."[38] It is at this level that it is possible to say with Tai-chu: "No bondage from the first, and what is the use of seeking emancipation? Act as you will, go on as you feel—without a second thought. This is the incomparable way."[39] Earlier Niu-t'ou had declared to his monks: "Even attaining Buddhahood must be regarded as an illness."[40]

In zazen the searching mind can easily be trapped in the circularity of thinking about no-thinking, which thoughtlessness (wu-hsin) can only be achieved by a break, a discontinuity, in the ordinary processes of taking thought. Like the insomniac who attempts to fall asleep through the device of counting sheep, if sleep comes it comes not as a fulfillment of the process, but as its exhaustion. As Yun-men warned: "Each of us carries a light within him, but when it is looked at it is turned into darkness."[41] No amount of striving and purposing can achieve the state of no-striving and no-purposing, just as one cannot, in the strictest sense, give oneself peace and tranquillity, which come instead when one has relinquished all effort that can only draw the strings of consciousness tighter. Though Zen aligns itself with the *jiriki* (self-power) approach rather than the *tariki* (other-power) approach—characteristic of the Jodo-shin-shu emphasis upon faith and grace through the salvation of Amida Buddha—spiritual realization is recognized as coming, not by self-effort as such, but ultimately by no-effort (*wu-wei*). This is not, however, seen as a boon bestowed from the otherness of some transcendent divine sphere, but as a self-manifestation of the Buddha-nature within oneself—and within all things.

The forty-first case of the *Wu-men-kuan* puts the matter bluntly, and in a style more characteristic of Zen:

> Bodhidharma sat facing the wall in meditation. The (future) Second Patriarch, who had been standing in the snow (waiting for an interview), cut off one of his arms (to demonstrate the sincerity of his seeking), and said: "My mind is not at peace. Master, pray pacify my mind." Bodhidharma replied, "Bring me your mind and I will pacify it!" Hui-k'o lamented: "I have searched for it, but cannot find it." Bodhidharma said simply: "There, I have pacified your mind."[42]

Similarly, Hui-k'o, after he became Bodhidharma's successor, was visited by a layman who said that he had been stricken with an illness by heaven because of his sin. He asked Hui-k'o to help him. Hui-k'o said, "If you can bring me your sin, I will repent for it." The layman responded, "(My) sin is not obtainable, though I have searched for it." Hui-k'o then said, "(There,) I have repented for your sin. . . . Live by the Buddha, the Dharma, and the Sangha."[43]

CHAPTER EIGHT

Socrates in China

Nan-chu'an: "Your body is unusually big;
isn't your straw hat too small?"

Huang-po: "Though my hat may be small,
the entire universe is within it."

TRANSMISSION OF THE LAMP

If the Zen master occasionally assimilates himself to the figure of the
clown-fool, or introduces certain comic motifs and stratagems, this
is not simply an end in itself, or even a personal actualization of
freedom alone, but also a means to an end. In full accord with the
Mahayanist emphasis upon the compassionate concern *(karuna)* of
the Bodhisattva for the enlightenment of all, the enlightened one seeks,
through a variety of techniques, including the *upaya* of humor and
clownishness, the awakening of the disciple. This approach has
similarities to the Holy Fool tradition in the Greek and Russian
Orthodox churches in which certain monks assumed the role of the
fool, and engaged in odd or impious behavior, in order to reveal the
folly of the people and awaken piety. The Zen master becomes
something of a fool and behaves or instructs in unconventional ways
in order to reveal the comedy in a false view of self and awaken a
new perspective on existence. In a real sense, he is, in Enid Welsford's
terms, the *punctum indifferens* and the fool as emancipator.

Precedent for this is already provided in the *Lankavatara Sutra*,
the favorite scripture of Bodhidharma, and therefore influential from
the earliest period of Zen in China. The *Lankavatara Sutra* refers
to certain Buddha-lands in which "Buddha-teaching is carried out by
mere gazing, or by the contraction of the facial muscles, or by the
raising of the eyebrows, by frowning or smiling, by clearing the throat,
by the twinkling of an eye, by merely thinking, or by a motion of

127

some kind."[1] This Buddha-land, thanks to a Zen facility for bringing everything, including Buddhas and Buddha-lands, down to earth, became in literal fact China, Korea, and Japan.

Hui-ts'ang, for example, asked one of his monks, "Can you get hold of Emptiness?" "I'll try," said the monk; and he cupped his hands in the air. "You haven't got anything in there!" Hui-ts'ang exclaimed. "Well, master," said the monk, "Please show me a better way." Thereupon Hui-ts'ang seized the monk's nose and gave it a hard yank. "Ouch!" yelled the monk, "you hurt me!" "That's the way to get hold of Emptiness!"[2]

Zen Midwifery

In this odd kind of relationship the master functions as a midwife of truth in the Socratic sense. And often this midwifery is of a comic sort, or has a comic dimension to it—though it may not be immediately apparent, as in the case of the painful tweaking of the monk's nose. The master does not and cannot teach the Truth in the sense of indoctrination; for the Truth to be realized—an inward, intuitive, non-discursive truth—cannot be dispensed in this way. It cannot, in fact, be dispensed in any way. When the wandering monk Tai-chu heard of the reputation of Master Ma-tsu, he went to study under him. Ma-tsu asked, "What do you expect to do by coming here?" "I have come to seek for the Buddha-dharma," he replied. Ma-tsu reprimanded him: "What do you mean by abandoning your own home? I have nothing in this place of mine. What kind of Buddha-dharma can you be seeking?"[3]

This, of course, presupposes that the Truth is present already, that one is already in the Truth, requiring only the proper moments or occasions for its realization. What is demanded, then, is not a method through which the master forces truths in to the mind of the disciple, but through which, as it were, the Truth is beaten out of him. Te-shan, in fact, was noted for a most equitable use of the stick on his disciples: whether they answered the master yes or no, whether they answered in any way or remained silent, they received thirty blows with the *keisaku*.[4]

The Truth, furthermore, is not only said to be within each

individual, which if left at that would seem to imply some unknown region that is to be explored and discovered, some place that one is to commence in search of. It is one's innermost and uttermost reality. The Sixth Patriarch, Hui-neng, whose teaching gave the definitive stamp to the subsequent history of Zen, expressed the point very dramatically: "Our original nature is Buddha, and apart from this nature there is no other Buddha. All the Buddhas of the past, present and future ages, and the twelve parts of the Scriptures, are immanent in the nature of man as its original endowment."[5]

Obviously, then, such a Truth cannot be given by one individual to another through some process of exchange, as one might pass coins from one purse to another. As Kuei-shan said, in refusing to attempt to give any answer to Chi-hsien: "Whatever I tell you will always be mine and will never concern you."[6] One can at most be awakened to the Truth which is already within, and from which one has never been separated; for it is what one really is in oneself. Such a Truth is necessarily inward and personal, not external and public. Chao-chou phrased the matter in terms of the "low comedy" for which Zen masters have justly been noted. Once when asked by a monk what he saw as the most important principle of Zen, he abruptly excused himself, saying, "I must now go to make water. Think, even such a trifling thing I have to do in person!"[7]

A critical term in Zen—and insofar as one can speak of a goal in Zen, the goal of Zen practice—is *kensho*, "seeing into one's nature." As Tai-hui pointedly insisted in one of his sermons: "The Truth is not what you hear from others or learn through understanding. Now keep yourself away from what you have seen, heard, and thought, and see what you have within yourself."[8] The Teacher therefore cannot teach the Truth to the learner as if a lecturer were transferring previously unknown information from lecture notes to the notebook of the disciple. By the same token, the Learner cannot learn the Truth; for it is a Truth which is already known and possessed, needing only to be *re*-cognized and *re*-alized. It is a Truth from which, in one sense, one has become estranged both in one's knowing and being, and yet a Truth from which in the final sense one cannot be and never has been divorced.

There is consequently also no direct path to this Truth, as if the seeker were in one place and the Truth elsewhere, with the problem being that of locating the Truth and making one's way toward it like a pilgrim along some well-established route. As the 16th-century Indian guru, Kabir, put it:

> Path presupposes distance;
> If he be near, no path needest thou at all.
> Verily it makes one smile
> To hear of a fish in water athirst.[9]

The Zen way can thus be no way at all; for all ways are at best tread-mills that permit the illusion of getting somewhere and learning something, and at worst endless detours which, if anything, get somewhere by proceeding further and further away. Thus Hui-chung responds to an inquisitive student: "If I am to answer your question now, there will be no end to it even if I continue till aeons are exhausted. The more one makes speeches, the further from the Tao one gets."[10] To avoid this is the way of indirection. This is not a way which goes anywhere, or even proposes to do so, but which offers the possibility of opening one's eyes and seeing where one really is in one's inwardness. In the words of the four-character phrase, *chao ku hua t'ou*, commonly exhibited on the meditation halls of Ch'an monasteries: "Turn inward the light on your self-nature."

The Truth that is to be communicated, then, cannot be communicated. It is not as if the master could hand everything over on a piece of paper which the monk could carry in his robe, or repeat in parrot-like fashion, or memorize and carry piously about along with the great variety of other bits of information, belief, and opinion in the drawers of the mind. Yun-men warned: "There are those who, upon seeing an old monk opening his mouth to speak, put his special words into their own mouths to chew them. They are like flies struggling to gobble up manure." Or again, "If I speak words to teach you so that you can, upon hearing them, understand, I shall in fact be throwing manure on your heads."[11] Thus, when a monk, seeking informational knowledge concerning the famed Nagarjuna—albeit a critical precursor of Zen, and the most important of the twenty-eight Indian Patriarchs claimed by the Zen sect—asked Yun-men, "What is the school of Nagarjuna?" Yun-men brusquely replied, "In India there are ninety-six classes of heretics, and you belong to the lowest!''[12]

Though the *Lankavatara Sutra* itself had defended the use of teachings and books for pointing and prodding in the right direction, at the same time it insisted on the constant dangers inherent in the substitution of propositional truths and abstract concepts for the Supreme Truth.

> Clinging to the external world, they cling to the study of books which are a means only, and do not know properly how to ascertain the truth of self-realization, which is Truth unspoiled by the four propositions. Self-realization is an exalted state of inner attainment which transcends all dualistic thinking and which is above the mind-system with its logic, reasoning, theorizing, and illustrations.[13]

The real Truth is that Truth in relation to which all other truths are seen, that all-embracing perspective upon existence which determines all other perspectives. This Truth, however, is not abstractly, but existentially realized. It is a mode of perception and of being, where knowing cannot be separated from being, which affects the whole of one's being and knowing. It is therefore not a Truth of the same order as all other truths, and cannot be appropriated as other truths can. For one does not in this instance see and experience any specific thing differently; rather one sees and experiences everything differently. The conclusion drawn from this in all mystical contexts, however carefully adhered to in method and in fact, has been that such a Truth cannot, in the nature of the case, be transmitted at all, if by transmission is meant the delivery of something to someone who formerly did not have it and now is about to receive it. This would be to make the teacher into a religious peddler rather than a spiritual guide. If the term ''communication'' is to be used at all, it can only refer to a process of provoking the ''learner'' to an awareness of that which is already understood. When the provincial minister came to inquire of Shen-hsiu of the Northern School concerning the essential Buddha-dharma, Shen-hsui responded:

> *The whole Buddha-Dharma*
> *Is inherent in one's own mind.*

131

Should one use mind to seek for it outside,
It is running away from one's father. [14]

Socrates struggled with the same problem in the *Meno*. If such a Truth were not previously known, why would it occur to anyone to seek for it; and if one seeks for it, how could it be communicated to him; and even if communicated, how could it be recognized as the Truth; and even if recognized as the Truth, how could it be inwardly received and appropriated as the Truth? If, then, the Truth is to be knowable it appears that in some sense it must already be known, and that the issue is primarily one of finding appropriate techniques and providing appropriate occasions by means of which the Truth can manifest itself. The fourth Patriarch Tao-hsin taught:

> Hundreds of thousands of dharmas are centered in the human heart. Wondrous virtues, numberless as the sands of the River Ganges, all exist in the source of the mind. All the gateways of discipline, meditation, wisdom, and supernatural manifestation are truly furnished by your mind. . .There is no triple world to escape from and no enlightenment to seek. . .Possessing such Dharma without deficiency, how could you differ from the Buddha? There is nothing other [than Buddha]. Simply act as freely as you wish; not engaging in any contemplation or discipline; not trying to make your heart pure and quiet; not raising ideas of greed or anger; and not harboring ideas of sorrow or anxiety. Striving after neither good conduct nor bad, let your behavior be as free as a vast flood. Whether you are walking, standing, sitting, or lying down, all that your eyes fall upon and all that you come across is [none other than] the activity of the Buddha. Then you are happy, free from anxiety, and your name is Buddha. [15]

The Comic Occasion

It is significant that Socrates is noted, not only for his insistence upon inwardness and the maeutic relationship, but for his use of various comic ploys, and his adoption of the roles of iconoclast and fool. Aristotle refers to Socrates as the ''mock-modest'' figure who, in his understatement and feigned ignorance, and in both his refusal to teach anything and insistence on having nothing to teach, was a troublesome

132

thorn in the side of the philosophical teachers and disputants of his day. Plato, also, though fearful of "violent laughter" and critical of clown performances as such, has Thrasymachus in the *Republic* call attention to the element of buffoonery in Socrates' "shamming ignorance" in an "imbecile way" to effect a realization of Truth. Socrates' role as "gadfly of Athens" and impious iconoclast was, in fact, to a significant extent that of the clown-fool's most profound and formidable form: one who has the disturbing capacity for bringing about the sudden remembrance of some understanding that lies buried beneath the sophistry of common discourse and doctrinaire pretension, even though he appears to be a simpleton who has nothing to offer, and from whom nothing is to be feared.

One is reminded in this of Ts'ao-shan's advice to his monks: "Keep your good deeds hidden and your function secret, that you may appear as a stupid and dull-witted man."[16] Master Tai-chu used to say to those who came to him for instruction: "I do not understand Zen, nor is there any special teaching to give out for your sake. Therefore, there is no need for you to be standing here for so long. It is best for you to get the matter settled within yourselves."[17] Similarly, the Sixth Patriarch, Hui-neng, when asked on what basis he succeeded the Fifth Patriarch, replied: "Because I do not understand Buddhism!"[18]

The Zen method of instruction, then, is first and foremost that of indirect communication. On the one hand this indirectness results from the insight that words, even in their attempt to point toward reality, have a special genius for clouding and concealing it, and blocking the fullness and clarity of the very experience to which they would point. In Tai-hui's letter to Miao-tsung he writes: "To talk about mind or nature is defiling; to talk about the unfathomable or the mysterious is defiling. . .to direct one's attention to it, to think about it is defiling; to be writing about it thus on paper with a brush is especially defiling."[19] Furthermore, because of the tendency of words to assume a kind of life of their own, there is a great concern in Zen over the possibility that—comedy of comedies—the seeker of spiritual food will somehow mistake a knowledge of the ingredients and a recitation of the recipe for the meal itself, or that, worse coming to worse, the cookbook will be eaten instead of the dinner.

Something of the old Taoist suspicion about words is also to be found in Zen. As the sage Chuang-tzu long before remarked: "The men of old took all they really knew with them to the grave. [Their words are] only the dirt they left behind."[20] Before him, Lao-tzu had prefaced the *Tao-teh-ching* (Book on the Power of the Tao) with a radical disclaimer: "The Tao that can be spoken [*taoed*] is not the true Tao; the Name that can be named is not the true Name."[21] This concern echoes and re-echoes in the Zen tradition. The venerable Kung-chi, responding to persistent questioning concerning the essence of the Tao and the Zen way said: "What can be named is not the great Tao, and what is either right or wrong is not Zen. If you wish to comprehend it, you will be using yellow leaves for coins in order to stop the crying of beggars."[22]

As Soren Kierkegaard rephrased the similar Socratic position, the master is not a teacher of truths, or one on whom the disciple is dependent for the truth, but merely an occasion for the Truth to manifest itself within the inner being of the disciple. This is the basis of his indirection. The master who offers himself on some other basis is a pretender and a deceiver. He sets up an external relationship to the Truth, and places the disciple in a state of attachment and bondage to himself, when no such dependence can ever be forthcoming as a condition for realizing the Truth. Though as Kierkegaard commented with characteristic wit: "While no human being was ever truly an authority for another, or ever helped anyone by posing as such, or was ever able to take his client with him in truth, there is another sort of success that may by such methods be won; for it has never yet been known to fail that one fool, when he goes astray, takes several others with him."[23] Socrates' conclusions from this are also those of Zen: the true master is a midwife. The midwife does not bring the baby, nor pass the baby from the stork to the mother, but assists the mother in delivering her own baby. Both the Truth and the condition for awakening it are present already, requiring only an occasion, or intervening cause, for its awakening.

Master Tao-lin had an attendant called Hui-t'ung who one day suddenly decided to leave him. The master asked him, "Where are you going?" The attendant replied, "Hui-t'ung became a monk for the sake of the dharma, but you, Venerable Sir, gave him no instruc-

134

tion at all. He now wishes to go here and there to learn the Buddha-dharma." The master said, "If such could be the Buddha-dharma, there is a little of it here also." The attendant asked, "Venerable Sir, what is your Buddha-dharma?" Tao-lin plucked a hair from his skin and blew it, whereupon Hui-t'ung "at last comprehended the profound message."[24]

The type of occasion afforded by the Zen master is frequently identified by the peculiarity of being a comic occasion. The comic occasion is, in fact, particularly suited to just such an indirection. A glance at some of the common features of comic lines, behavior, or situations reveals the close analogy between comic techniques and Zen techniques, as well as the serviceability of comic techniques in Zen: irrationality, contradiction, incongruity, absurdity, irrelevancy, triviality, nonsense, distortion, abruptness, shock, sudden twist, reversal, overturning. In both comedy and Zen one is prevented from drawing a purely intellectual conclusion at the end of an argument, and therefore entering the abstractness and deceptiveness of a pseudo-appropriation of the truth. The possibility of such an external relationship to the truth is short-circuited. This is delightfully illustrated in the tale of the first Ch'an master to visit Tibet. As was the custom, he was invited to participate in the traditional Tibetan debate which tests and displays not simply the dialectical skill, but the spiritual understanding of the monk. When the Tibetan monk, chosen to debate with the Ch'an master, had forcefully completed his opening challenge, the Ch'an master slowly rose before the hushed assembly and, after making the appropriate bows, without a word disrobed. Having thus revealed the "naked truth" he sat down. The debate was ended![25]

The comic line or gesture actually goes nowhere and, in a literal sense, teaches nothing. Instead it calls everything to an abrupt halt. In a joke, for instance, the story seems to be getting somewhere for a time; the tale unfolds smoothly and rationally; information follows information in plausible order; and then, suddenly, the humorous twist throws everything into confusion. Instead of the story arriving at some reasonable conclusion or climax, the whole intellectual progression collapses. Yet it is just such a collapse that is the necessary antecedent to the manifestation of another order of truth—whether in comedy or in Zen.

Many tales have arisen in the Zen tradition illustrating the use of such maeutic devices. A monk asked Ts'ao-shan, "Are not monks persons of great compassion?" The master indicated approval. "Suppose the six bandits come at them. What should they do?" "Also be compassionate," the master replied. The monk pressed further: "How is one to be compassionate?" The master said, "Wipe them out with one sweep of the sword!" "What then?" asked the monk. "Then they will be harmonized."[26] Through this word-play the monk is supposed to see through the incongruity of a literal interpretation, that the six bandits are the sensuous desires which must be both "wiped out" and at the same time harmonized. More importantly, he must come to the realization that the moral of the mondo is really no moral, that the master's enigmatic reply is a refusal to moralize in the abstract. The humorous evasion of the problem as posed is a rejection of the terms of the question; for what is needed is not some prefabricated set of rules and recommendations for behavior, which can easily lead to the illusion that to perform acts defined as compassionate is identical with being compassionate. The master comically distorts and confounds the issue as stated, for clearly the problem is not to arrive at a rational description of compassionate acts, but to become compassionate.

Chih-chang one day announced a lecture on the exemplary virtues of the Bodhisattva Kuan-yin. After his monks had assembled he said, "When you have listened to the deeds of Kuan-yin you are able to behave properly in accordance with circumstances." The monks, on hearing no further elaboration, asked, "What are the deeds of Kuan-yin?" The master simply snapped his fingers; "Do you all hear that?" The monks indicated that they had. "This nonsensical company of yours; what do you want to get by coming here?" So saying, Chih-chang drove them from the hall with his stick and, laughing heartily, returned to his quarters.[27]

One of the most unusual features of Zen teaching is its ingenious and frequent use of plays upon words, ideas, and situations—though to deal with them in any detail would require cumbersome notations on the nuances and idioms of the Chinese and Japanese languages and cultures. Suffice it to note the profusion itself of puns, idiomatic turns upon words, paradoxes and enigmatic sayings, startling gestures and acts. All have the same general intent of calling an abrupt halt to an unenlightened plane of perception, and projecting the hearer onto a more fundamental plane of experience. The disciple is never allowed to rest in an intellectual understanding or an attachment to names and forms. All such effort is kept in constant turmoil. This violation of ordinary meaning and rationality is of the same order and intent as the many other forms of Zen violence: the *keisaku*, the slap, the kick, the shout, and the loud roar of laughter. The problem, as Fa-yen put it, is that "reality is right before you [and within you]; yet you are apt to translate it into a world of names and forms. How are you going to re-translate it into its original?"[28]

Koan Nonsense and Mondo Playfulness

Behind this peculiar dialogical method of Zen lies the game of debate itself, with its premium upon cleverness, competitiveness and wit, and the demonstration of mastery through verbally defeating one's opponent—as in the confirmation of maturity and wisdom in Tibetan Buddhism through dialectical skill, or in the Chinese Buddhist custom that a travelling monk may stay at a monastery if he bests a resident monk with the last word in debate. Much of this emphasis upon dialectical agility is to be found in Zen, as in the numerous tales of the meeting of two Zen masters, testing one another's enlightenment in what appears to be a "Can you top this?" series of riddles, double-entendres, non-sequiturs, and ejaculations. In some accounts, in fact, the dialogue is purely playful, as in the contest proposed by Chao-chou one leisurely summer day to his attending disciple, Wen-yuan. The object was to see who could "identify himself with the lowest thing in the scale of human values." The winner was to pay the loser a cake. Chao-chou began: "I am the ass's feces." Wen-yuan: "I am a worm in the feces." Chao-chou, unable to think of a rejoinder, asked: "What are you doing there?" Replied Wen-yuan, "I am spending my summer vacation!" Chao-chou conceded defeat.[29]

This in itself should not be taken as detracting from the method, for one must be careful not to make the role of games and humorous repartee only a serious one. Is it not permissible that even Zen masters should laugh and play? Otherwise we are only confronted with a new form of bondage to seriousness and a new reduction to utilitarianism, neither of which reflect the joyful freedom of enlightenment. The dialectical method as a method is, in fact, the invitation to this higher freedom beyond technique and utility, beyond seriousness and purpose, beyond means and ends. Rather than laughter and play representing the lowest level of attainment, they represent the highest; and the method moves toward rather than away from the spirit which they symbolize.

Even as method, there is a distinct element of play and of game in the dialogues between master and disciple, many of which move back and forth at length, like the thrusts in a fencing match, with each maneuver by the disciple being deftly countered in an effort to bring him to the point at which his resources are exhausted and he is opened (cut open!) to deeper insight. Whether this is the play and game of humor or not—though one suspects that behind the awesome visage of the master there is a twinkle in the eye of one who participates in a higher knowledge, and thus who will very likely laugh loudly when the final blow is administered—the purpose of the wit and repartee is not to develop the dialectical abilities of the disciple. Nor is it to display those of the master. Rather it is to reveal the rational approach as well as a false trail. The master plays with the disciple, like a cat with a mouse, not however to destroy him but to awaken him, and to bring him to that level where he responds, not mechanically or even cleverly, but spontaneously out of his self-nature. Instead of the mondo being an exercise in sophistry, leading nowhere, it is really an exercise in what might fittingly be called a comedy of errors. Once the error is revealed the disciple realizes how awkward and artificial his clumsy reponses have been, or how funny the question he has raised—as in the case of the monk who asked Ch'ang-ch'ing, "What is meant by the True Eye of the Law?" only to receive the reply, "I have a favor to ask of you: don't throw dirt around!"[30]

Similarly, in the last case of the *Wu-men-kuan* the tale is related of the monk who asked Master Ch'ien-feng, "There is only one road to Nirvana, and yet there are ten quarters of Buddha-land. Where is the true path?" Ch'ien-feng raised his walking stick to draw a horizontal line in the air: "Here." On another occasion the same

138

question was asked of Master Yun-men, who held up his fan and replied: "This fan jumps up to the thirty-third heaven and hits the presiding deity on the nose, then comes down to the Eastern Sea and hits the holy carp. The carp becomes a dragon, which brings a flood of rain."[31] Both answers are, of course, "correct"!

In the same vein many of the paradoxical and seemingly nonsensical koans, given to the disciple to meditate upon as a way of gaining release from an unenlightened way of perceiving the self and the world, have a comic dimension to them. This is not accidental, for the very provenance of comedy is nonsense and absurdity. Comedy plays with absurdity and revels in irrationality, turning it to its own ends. E.R. Hughes, in his analysis of epistemological methods in Chinese philosophy, notes that "of all paradoxical writing in Chinese literature—and there is a good deal—the most paradoxical is that of the Ch'an Buddhist; and. . .I mean consciously and deliberately paradoxical, even with the intention of causing laughter, to make evident the incongruities in the human situation."[32]

In this Zen employment of contradiction and nonsense is to be found considerable psychological insight. One may approach a false view of things by rationally pointing out its errors and cul-de-sacs in the grand manner of the philosopher; but often a more effective method is to do so absurdly and humorously. For once the ridiculousness of the viewpoint is revealed and appropriated comically, instead of having been driven into a corner and held at bay by the overpowering logic of the master—as in the *reductio ad absurdum* methodology pursued in the Madhyamika system of Nagarjuna—one has been freed to laugh. On the other hand, there is the distinct possibility in the discursive approach that the disciple will be tempted by the very intellectualism of the approach to seek some new way of overcoming the philosophical dilemma, some nuance that has been omitted or some angle that has been overlooked by the master—a tantalizing defeat which may only perpetuate the argument, and hence the deception, *ad infinitum.* Something of the spirit and wisdom of the Zen method is captured in the account of Yang-ch'i, who rose ostensibly to lecture to his monks on the path of enlightenment, but instead began laughing and exclaimed simply, "Ha! ha! ha! What's all this! Go to the back of the hall and have some tea!"[33]

It is because of this comic/socratic character of the Zen technique that one finds such a constant stress in the koan and mondo upon contradiction, nonsense, and absurdity—or at least apparent contradiction, nonsense, and absurdity. As in Yun-men's answer to the searching question of the monk, "When all mental activity is at an end, what is it like?"—"Bring the Buddha-hall here, and we'll weigh it together!"[34]—it is as if one were suddenly plunged into the world of Lear's nonsense rhymes or of Alice in Wonderland. It is not, however, sheer nonsense. A truth is being pointed to obliquely and comically, for to point to it directly and philosophically would be both impossible and misleading. Nonsense does not mean totally without sense, but without sense in the customary view of the sensical, and beyond rationality in the ordinary understanding of reason. In nonsense one refuses to take with absolute seriousness—with humorlessness—the world of sense, whether of common sense or sophisticated reason. Nonsense is the question mark placed after the supposedly firm reality of the world of intelligibility, the irrefutable logic of rationality, or the categories and dichotomies of any system. It is this maeutic play upon irrationality in order to move beyond rationality that is expressed in Hakuin's familiar koan, "What is the sound of one hand clapping?" or in Yun-men's reply to the question, "What is a sermon that surpasses the teaching of the Buddha and the Patriarchs?" "Cake!"[35]

Many of the cryptic sayings of the masters do, of course, carry a great deal of symbolic freight. But even here, though they may be said to be filled with meaning, their enigmatic form is designed to mystify and thwart and therefore cut short ordinary processes of discrimination and appropriation. When the meaning becomes clear, it is not meaning in the sense of common rationality, and it refuses to be "grasped" in such terms. A great deal of Buddhist teaching is here tightly compressed in the small chambers of the riddle or pun or gibberish in readiness, as it were, for the explosion and burst of insight that must occur, and which in this manner is to be tested or expressed.

Very early in its development Zen distinguished itself from other Buddhist sects in China through the substitution of the much more "socratic" mondo and koan method of teaching for the sutra method, introduced from India, of recitation and exposition of scriptures and aphorisms. The sutra method easily lent itself to memorization, interpretation, and intellectual appropriation, but not necessarily enlightenment; whereas the dialogical and dialectical method of Zen constantly demanded interiorization. Superficial, and essentially external, processes of assimilation were systematically frustrated. The Truth had to be appropriated inwardly and discovered in inwardness, or it could not be appropriated at all. It is thus that the scholar Te-shan came, with his knapsack full of Ch'ing-lung's commentaries on the *Vajracchedika*, to a Zen mountain retreat to engage the monks in debate, intending to dispute and discredit Zen, only to remain as a disciple, and to consign his books to the flames. According to the Zen records he said in explanation of his act: "An exhaustive discussion of the abstruse is like a hair thrown into the infinite void; and the fullest exertion of all capabilities is like a little drop of water falling into an unfathomable gulf."[36]

It is difficult to imagine the word-oriented Near Eastern religions, with their stress upon the Word of creation, the prophetic Word, the biblical Word, the incarnate Word, the kerygmatic Word, and preaching the Word, including in their lists of holy persons one who demonstrated spiritual understanding by burning the scriptures, whether Torah, Gospels, or Qur'an—although there have been numerous instances of burning other peoples' books and bibles. In a very real sense in Zen, as in mysticism generally, inner illumina-tion implies the burning of all words. The Word of scripture or of reason is at most only an occasion for the manifestation of that "wordless Dharma" which is beyond all words. In relation to this Dharma even the most sacred words stand in the awkwardness of hiding and obstructing that which they would reveal. The final word is silence, pregnant with meaning.

The comic/socratic character of Zen pedagogy is also apparent in the unusual prominence and extensive employment of a large body of anecdotal literature (the source of most of the koan and mondo materials)—anecdotes which have a distinctively mundane, common-place, and humorous cast, and which function as a kind of Zen scripture and meditation manual. Anecdotal materials, to be sure, may be found in any tradition. But in Zen the role of the anecdote is much more central to the teaching and point of the teaching. The Zen tradi-

141

tion is not disseminated through a heavily symbolic ritual, or creed and confession, or scriptural canon, or catechetical indoctrination, or theological, dogmatic, or philosophical disputation—all so familiar to Western religion. In the West the anecdote stands far more toward the periphery of the tradition, as a matter of popular discourse, sermonic illustration, ante-room banter, and the like. It is not at the heart of the teaching, either in terms of method or content, but is a kind of concession to those unable to ascend the lofty heights of theological, philosophical, and ethical discourse. In Zen, however, the reverse is closer to its peculiar genius. Without a focus on scripture, liturgy, myth, doctrine, or metaphysics, the anecdote is more an official organ than an appendage. Rather than being a vehicle for popularization, it points instead to that level of understanding and awareness that lies beyond all symbol, gesture and word, all reason and belief, even the most sophisticated.

The four largest collections of anecdotal materials indicate something of the extensiveness and importance of this remarkable "scripture": *The Transmission of the Lamp* (1004) in 14 folios; *Five Lamps Meeting at the Source* (960-1279) in 20 folios; *A Finger Pointing at the Moon* (1602) in 10 folios; and *The Imperial Collection of Ch'an Sayings* (1723-35) in 14 folios. The very uniqueness of this anecdotal literature is in itself suggestive of the spirit and character of Zen. Given this kind of prominence, it is not surprising that, if for this reason alone, humor is also prominent in Zen. For though anecdotes are not necessarily humorous, they are often so. In the very humanness, the everydayness, the give-and-take of the tales of Zen masters and their disciples, the anecdote is much more likely to involve a dimension of the comic than any other mode of religious discourse.

It might, of course, be a temptation to suppose that, because of the relative simplicity and good humor of the Zen stories, one has understood Zen in understanding the stories. The peculiarity of Zen anecdotes in general, however, is the same peculiarity as that of the koan and mondo in particular. Unlike the anecdotes to be found in most other religious traditions, there is usually no simple moral or lesson to be drawn from them which could conveniently be tucked away in the folds of an intellectual understanding, except the conclusion that there is no moral code or doctrinal lesson forthcoming.

If the expectation is otherwise, one listens to the anecdote either with the pretense of understanding or with the same consternation, the same intellectual despair, the same sense of being logically short-circuited, the same feeling of being cheated or left hanging in mid-air, as in being confronted with a koan as such. It is as if the entire anecdotal tradition were a big joke played on all anticipations of an easy mental comprehension and superficial appropriation. One sits down to what appears to be a plate of succulent and readily digestible fish, and receives instead a stone. Thus Master Tao-ch'in responded to the question, "What is the Tao?" by saying, "There are carpfish on the mountain and raspberries in the dirt at the bottom of the river."[37]

Even Shakespeare's fool, Bottom, understood the problem.

> I have had a most rare vision. I have had a dream, past the wit of man to say what dream it was. Man is but an ass if he go about to expound this dream. Methought I was—there is no man can tell what. Methought I was, and methought I had; but man is but a patch'd fool if he will offer to say what methought I had. The eye of man hath not heard, the ear of man hath not seen, man's hand is not able to taste, his tongue to conceive, nor his heart to report, what my dream was. I will get Peter Quince to write a ballad of this dream. It shall be call'd "Bottom's Dream," because it hath no bottom...
>
> A MIDSUMMER NIGHT'S DREAM IV.i.

Though words cannot fathom or contain the vision that has no bottom, this should not be taken to imply that the words of the Buddha or of the master's teaching do not have an important place and function. Zen masters have always used sutras, given instruction, delivered sermons. Everything is not done cryptically and koanically. Dogen warned his monks about excessive disparaging of scriptures and teachings. "It is a big mistake to think that the scriptures and treatises are unimportant because they are concessional forms of the Dharma and therefore no more than paintings of rice cakes."[38] As forms of the Dharma they are not alien to the Dharma or other than the Dharma. One must be careful not to establish a new dualism, between true Dharma and a paper Dharma, or between the Buddha and the words of the Buddha. A particular teaching may be limited, partial, and reducible to empty words; but as that which expresses the Truth and points to the Truth it is not other than the Truth or foreign to the Truth. There should be no duality between the Truth of the Dharma and the truths of the Dharma, no antagonism between recipe and rice cake. One needs both the recipe and the cake. Says Dogen, "If the Buddha Dharma is real, then the picture of the rice cake is real, too."[39]

CHAPTER NINE

Getting the Point of the Joke

*When the approach to enlightenment is like the swift thrust
of a sword to the center of all things, then both worldliness
and saintliness are completely eliminated, and true reality
is revealed.*

KUEI-SHAN

In the emphasis upon "sudden awakening," found in the Southern
Ch'an school of Hui-neng, is to be seen a further point of
correspondence between humor and Zen. Common to both is the
element of abruptness, in the one case an abruptness which precipitates
laughter, in the other case an abruptness which precipitates awakening.
As has already been intimated, what the Zen masters have often done
is to use the one form of abruptness as an occasion for the other.

This relationship is by no means accidental, since the sudden
realization of the point of a joke is analogous to the sudden realization of enlightenment, as this is interpreted by Hui-neng and Lin-chi.
The point of the joke, or the humorousness in the antics of the clown
or fool, is something that is caught immediately and effortlessly, or
it is not caught at all. It does, of course, require preparation in terms
of setting, context, and mood—and here, as it were, the "sudden
realization" school of Zen includes rather than excludes the
"progressive realization" school. Nothing is more awkward and flat
than an inappropriate joke, or a joke out of the context that permitted
it to be funny, or a joke the surprise ending of which has not been
carefully prepared. But when the comic twist comes, like the "twist"
of enlightenment, it comes spontaneously and uncoerced. If it requires
explanation and the effort of understanding it ceases to be funny, even
when it is comprehended intellectually, and the attempt is made to
force an embarrassed smile. If one does not get the point
instantaneously and intuitively, laughter does not follow—i.e., it is

145

not funny—though later one may come to understand the humor in it in a second-handed, discursive understanding.

The Explosion of Truth

Similarly, in the word tests of the disciple, or the verbal debates of the monks and masters, only the answer that is instantaneously, effortlessly, and spontaneously given is acceptable, not the answer that follows the pause of reflection and reasoning, let alone a premeditated response, no matter how clever or ingenious it might be. Such could not represent a trans-rational insight or the intuitive perception of truth. A deliberated or rehearsed reply is evidence against rather than for the immediate plane of understanding that is here being solicited and tested—even though rehearsed replies and books of previously accepted answers are not unknown in Zen monasteries. Realization comes when it comes, and manifests itself when occasion demands, in a *ksana'* instant—*ksana'* being an expression for the smallest measure of time. It is the moment, that is to say, without temporal duration, the moment which immediately and spontaneously proceeds from the self-nature. One can prepare for it in a limited sense, as one sets the stage for the point of a joke. But the preparation itself does not achieve the *ksana'* instant, which happens almost as if, like a comic perception and abrupt burst of laughter, it were unrelated or absurdly related to its preparation. Such a moment intersects time; it bursts into time; but it is not a continuation or elongation of the temporal process. It is not attached to the past or future; it is the moment which opens out into eternity.

This is not to negate the importance of careful preparation, whether through zazen practice or the instruction of the master or the guidance of the sutras. Lu K'uan Yu argues that the koan, for example, is properly used in relation to those disciples "whose minds are already disentangled from illusions and whose potentialities are activated to the full, ready to absorb the truth."[1] There is a difference between a ripe and unripe consciousness. Clearly the Zen masters, in using various techniques of indirect communication, presupposed some familiarity with the larger Buddhist tradition, and some inclination to move in the direction of its concerns and insights. They did not shout and laugh and kick in a vacuum. All effort and anticipation, however, involve the real danger of forfeiting the conclusion which, in a strict sense, does not follow from what has preceded it. If it were otherwise, the perception would not be a new and revolutionary perception, but a continuation, however refined and perfected, of the old. Master Tai-chu put the matter very simply, quoting a sutra: "The perception of Buddha-nature depends on the right moment, the direct cause [the seed of Buddhahood within], and the intervening cause [the precipitating occasion]. When the time is ripe, one is like a deluded man who is suddenly awakened and who has forgotten all about something which he suddenly remembers. Only then can his be the self-possessed (nature) which does not come from without."[2]

Like comic appreciation, spiritual awakening has a *non sequitur* character about it. It comes spontaneously and uncoerced by anything that might attempt to give it birth. Hence both the Taoist and Zen emphases upon no-effort and no-striving (*wu-wei*) which is easily confused with the counsels of a do-nothing party, or the advice of advocates of a cheap and easy enlightenment. Nan-chu'an was once asked by Chao-chou, "What is Tao?" "Ordinary mind is Tao," he replied. "Should we try to get it?" Chao asked. "As soon as you try, you miss it." "How do we know without trying?" Chao pressed further. Nan-chu'an responded: "Tao is beyond both knowing and not knowing. Knowing is false perception and not knowing is lack of awareness. When one attains to Tao it is certain that one will see it as clearly as one sees the vastness of the universe. Then what is the use of arguing about it?"[3]

The comic spirit, therefore, is not only analogous to, but akin to, the intuitive spirit that is central to Zen. In contradistinction to rationalism and empiricism, in both Zen and the comic sense there is involved an intuition which not only directly perceives the truth, but does so immediately, and therefore dispenses with the construction of elaborate arguments and evidences which only postpone understanding indefinitely. One either grasps the point instantly or not, which is something no amount of discussion of itself can effect. There is, of course, the case of the proverbial Englishman who gets the point of the joke and laughs a day later. Nevertheless, the delayed comprehension of the joke comes, when it comes, abruptly and

147

spontaneously. Explaining a joke, therefore, like explaining enlightenment, is the worst thing that could happen to it. For the rational translation of its non-rationality is totally different from getting the significance immediately and naturally—that is, from actually experiencing its humorousness. In the one case it is intellectualized, and though the point may be comprehended nobody laughs, indeed is prevented from laughing except in a nervous attempt at imitating the appropriate response. In the other case the laughter is not the result of purposively taking thought about the matter, and everybody laughs naturally and effortlessly.

The immersion in the immediacy of the moment in laughter is thus of the same order as the Zen emphasis upon entering and living within the Eternal Now. The moment of comic awareness is not a matter of reflection upon some process. There is no looking backward into the past or forward to the future, no retrospection or anticipation. Such a moment is free from the dissection of analysis, and free from nostalgic attachment to the past or anxious attachment to the future. The moment which belongs to comedy and laughter is the present instant. To participate in comic insight is to participate in the immediacy and spontaneity of the Now. It is not an argument going somewhere or having been somewhere, but a procession brought to a sudden halt and plunged into the laughter of eternity.

It is for this reason that humor and Zen are so suited to each other, and in their spheres of coincidence so inseparable. Getting the point of a joke, or seeing things in comic perspective, like getting the "point" of Zen, is something that cannot be reached either in strictly rationalist or empiricist terms, while smiling or laughing is a sign that one has moved beyond a mere discursive comprehension to a genuine understanding. Thus when Wen Chen-ching was asked, "Who is the Buddha?" he laughed most heartily. The puzzled monk was taken aback: "I do not see why my question makes you laugh so." Wen replied, "I laugh at your attempt to get into the meaning by merely following the letter."[4] Here the laughter of the master calls an abrupt halt to the false path being taken by the disciple, and invites him to a similar laughter with respect to the folly of his approach to the problem. If the point of the laughter is perceived, and if he too can begin to laugh, he will have already entered the true path.

The relationship was, in fact, suggested in the *Lankavatara Sutra*: "The discriminating-mind [*mano-vijnana*] is a dancer and a magician with the objective world as his stage. Intuitive-mind [*manas*] is the wise jester who travels with the magician and reflects upon his emptiness and transiency."[5] Herein is the clue to the jester-like triviality of so many koans and mondos, a triviality of the same sort as that in which comedy indulges. In answer to the classic Zen question as to the meaning of Bodhidharma's coming from the West, Fo-chien replied: "When you taste vinegar you know it is sour, and when you taste salt you know it is salty"; San-sheng remarked, "Tainted meat collects flies"; and Hsing-hua retorted, "On the back of a broken-down donkey there are already enough flies!"[6]

Similarly the element of apparent irrelevancy is another characteristic of the master's response to the monk's questions, a logical *non sequitur* which challenges the capacity of reason for solving the problem—as in Tung-shan Shou-ch'u's response to the question, "What is the nature of the Buddha?": "Three pounds of hemp!"[7] Like the comic employment of irrelevant speech or action, the whole scene is suddenly set in a radically different light. The normal train of thought and expectation is caught up short; it is interrupted and baffled; and one is forced to appropriate the situation in a different manner. A jester's trick has been played on the discriminating mind (*mano-vijnana*) by the intuitive-mind (*manas*), and consciousness is opened up to the moment in which a deeper awareness can break through. When a monk asked Chao-chou "If all things return to the one, to what does the one return?" The master replied, "I had a linen robe made in Ch'ing State; it weighs seven pounds."[8]

It should not, of course, be assumed that such Zen techniques always work. While the anecdotal records usually give cases where the technique has been successful, they are also remarkably candid in including a number of cases where the point was not gotten. The story is told of Nan-chu'an that he once went into the vegetable garden and, finding a monk there, the master picked up a tile and threw it at him. When the monk turned around in surprise, Nan-chu'an raised his foot. The startled monk made no response, and the master returned to his quarters. The monk in consternation followed Nan-chu'an into his quarters, pleading for an answer: "Just now, Master, you threw a tile at me and it struck me. Why was I not enlightened?'' Nan-chu'an asked in return, ''Why did I raise my foot?'' The monk still did not understand.[9]

The Comic Twist

A correlation is also to be seen in the methodology of Zen ''midwifery'' between the elements of suddenness, surprise, and shock in the comic twist and the similar effect of the blow of the *keisaku*, as well as the slapping, kicking, and shouting for which Zen masters have been notorious. These are all abrupt teaching (*tun chiao*) methods of the same order and intent. Comic techniques are among these several forms of spiritual ''shock therapy'' which serve to break up the patterns of thought that hold the individual in bondage. At a certain juncture further words and reasonings may only bind the cords more tightly, or perpetuate the illusion that the problem is solvable in these terms. What may be required instead is the sudden jolt of the koan, the irrational turn of the humorous anecdote, or the absurdity of the comic figure or gesture. If the individual has lost touch with the true nature of things, and is caught in a web of artificial constructs, the function of humor can be that of snapping the bonds of illusion and restoring reality.

The advantage and intent of such methods is summed up in Yuan-wu's succinct comment on the *koan* in the *Pi-yen-lu*: ''There is no crack in which to insert their intellectual teeth.''[10] Thus when Hsiang-yen's man, hanging precariously from a tree limb by his teeth, is called upon to ''Speak!'' there is no either/or which dramatically presents itself for some heroic ethical or religious decision, but a comic absurdity which thwarts any attempt at coming to terms with the situation through the ordinary channels of intellection and decision-making. Both alternatives are rendered impossible, forcing the resolution onto another plane. The choice, however, between a dramatic form of abruptness and a more comic form is a matter of accommodating the technique to the situation and individual involved, in full accord with the ancient practice among Indian and Asian spiritual masters of adjusting the approach to the specific personality and need of the individual. Most commonly, the comic and dramatic approaches are used side-by-side, as counterpoint to each other. This is the effect of the humorous title Genro gives to his 18th-century collection of one hundred koans: *Tetteki Tosui*, or the *Solid Iron Flute Blown Upside Down*.[11] The caption itself indicates the folly in all claims to an intellectual attainment of the wisdom toward which the koans in the anthology point. What could be more clownishly absurd than the picture of a musician standing on his head, blowing on what turns out to be a solid iron flute, with his eyes bulging and cheeks bursting in dogged determination? And yet this, in the Zen view of it, is a fitting symbol for the common folly of attempting to "grasp" reality through the instruments of the discriminating-mind. There must, therefore, be a frustration and confounding of the intellect, so that its normal procedures will be checked and its insistence on dominating the scene and calling all tunes will be undercut. There must be an abdication of the lordship of reason which assigns everything to its place in the abstract system, saying to one "go here" and to another "go there." There must be a defeat of that rational imperialism which insists on possessing and governing all things as objects of its thought, yet which ends up the prisoner of its own empire. Proud reason must be made to appear in its comic patchwork and motley colors, with the dialectician as dunce, and the theoretician as dupe. The nimble wit, which has confidently and yet anxiously leapt about, must be made to do what it will inevitably do: fall flat on its face. There must be a collapse of some kind.

Hakuin's commentary on the *Hannya Shingyo*, which he entitled *Dokugo* ("poisonous words of") *Hannya Shingyo*, is illustrative of just such a collapse. The text is unusual indeed by comparison with most commentaries on sacred scripture. Under the pretense of praising and interpreting the sutra, Hakuin in fact abuses it, advising the reader to, in his words,

> Throw this luxuriant entangling growth
> That fills all the sky
> Over all the great monks of the Four Seas and Five Lakes,
> And tie them up.[12]

The shock-value of this wry humor—on the surface sacrilegious—is it's own justification as a device for awakening the reader to the pitfalls inherent in a mere intellectual and doctrinal acceptance of any religious teaching, however revered: that it may be substituted for the reality toward which it points, like "mistaking the pointing finger for the moon."[13] Or, as in the third case of the *Wu-men-kuan*, it may be a mistaking of the pointing finger of Zen for Zen. Chu-ti, whenever asked a question about Zen, would only reply by raising his finger. His attendant, therefore, when once asked about his master's doctrine, which he assumed to be admirably summed up in the master's gesture, aped his master in reply, and lifted a finger. When Chu-ti learned of this, he cut off the boy's finger. While the boy screamed in pain, Chu-ti again lifted his finger, and the boy was enlightened.[14]

Such was the insistence of the *Lankavatara Sutra* itself, which says of its own doctrines: "These teachings are only a finger pointing toward Noble Wisdom [*prajna*]. . .So with the teachings in all the sutras. They are intended for the consideration and guidance of the discriminating-minds [*mano-vijnana*] of all people; but they are not the truth itself, which can only be self-realized within one's deepest consciousness."[15] So seriously are the warnings of this sutra taken that, from earliest times, as Lu K'uan Yu comments, "Ch'an masters rarely used those Buddhist terms found in all sutras. For men are always prone to cling to the terminology which, in their quest for more learning and wider knowledge, can only stimulate their faculties of thought and intensify their discriminations."[16] This, in Yun-men's blunter way of putting it, would simply be to "swallow the saliva of other people, and succeed in memorizing and accumulating heaps and loads of curios and antiques."[17]

In this lies the simple (yet by no means easy) realization that the problem may be aggravated rather than resolved by any further pile-up of words and distinctions, however much Buddhist sutras indulge in them. It is better, in a sense, to be attached even to physical objects and sensuous delights than the often self-contained and self-perpetuating and in themselves unreal conceptualizations of the mind. To circumvent this last retreat may require some shocking and impious act, as in the case of Hsiang-yen who, having studied his many sutras to no avail, burned all his books and became a wandering monk, saying, "A cake drawn on paper can never satisfy hunger." Shortly thereafter, as he was one day collecting grass at the ruins of a monastery, he picked up a broken tile and tossed it away. It struck a stalk of bamboo with a ping, and on hearing the sound he was instantly awakened, and began laughing heartily.[18]

The Whole World Taken by Surprise

The place of the comic in Zen may thus be viewed as parallel to the two views of the place of painting in Zen: as a technique for spiritual realization, and as the expression of spiritual realization. It is not that one necessarily sees the situation as particularly humorous initially, or is anticipating a comic twist. Generally not; one is dead serious— which, in fact, turns out to be part of the problem. Enlightenment may have been sought through scrutiny of the sutras, pious acts, or long hours of meditation. One may have wrestled in dialogue with the master, or attempted—with intense concentration—to solve the insoluble koan one has been given. Perhaps one has been repeatedly rebuffed in *sanzen* sessions with the master, who has rejected every solution. The situation builds to a climax. The tension is seemingly unbearable. A breaking point is reached. Then the release comes, suddenly and simply. One escapes the vicious circle of striving and grasping; and the tight hold of the ego and the intellect is relaxed— often through the unexpected intervention of a miscellaneous event, like a tile falling off the roof, or Basho's frog jumping into the pond. As K'ung-ku defined it, a *satori* is a "grand overturning of the whole system of consciousness."[19] Or as Wu-men wrote concerning satori in his commentary on the first case of the *Wu-men-kuan*: "When the time comes for a final explosion, the result will resemble the whole world being taken by surprise."[20]

Humor and laughter in Zen pedagogy, therefore, are not as extraneous as might appear at first hearing. For the elements of absurdity and surprise are the hallmarks of the comic twist and comic perception. Laughter is an explosive response to a situation which has suddenly been plunged into a contradiction or reduced to an absurdity. Yet out of that absurdity has come an unexpectedly different way of perceiving and responding to life. We commonly laugh in response to gaining some new insight into things, or solution to a perplexity, or resolution of a conflict. In laughter we reprimand ourselves with, "Why didn't I think of that before?" Or we exclaim over our dullness in not having seen a truth that seems so simple and obvious and natural, a truth that has stood before us all the while, waiting for us merely to open our eyes to see it. We laugh at our former foolishness and blindness in the light of this new realization, a laughter which also signifies our gratitude for the freedom from our former ignorance, and our enjoyment of the new being and new understanding that is ours. Hence, as R.H. Blyth has also suggested, "enlightenment is frequently accompanied by laughing of a transcendental kind, which may further be described as a laughter of surprised approval."[21]

An early Buddhist controversy arose over the question whether the Buddha, who had been credited by the sutras with having smiled on several occasions, smiled on seeing the subtle and sublime truth of enlightenment, or on seeing the foolishness and ludicrousness of the unenlightened. On the mutually accepted assumption that the source of smiling or laughter was the pleasurable, the issue was joined as to whether this pleasure in the case of the Buddha arose from observing the most exalted beauty and truth, or ugliness and error. It was Buddhadatta's thesis in the *Abhidhammavatara* that the true source of the Buddha's smile was the degraded (*anulara*), not the subtle (*anolarika*), though not necessarily in the Hobbesian sense of a feeling of "glory arising from a sudden conception of some eminency in ourselves by comparison with the infirmity of others." Rather, Buddhadatta argued, it was a smile in the sense of the Buddha's exultation over escaping the bonds of ignorance and desire, and a subsequent perception of their folly.[22] Yet this seems unnecessarily restrictive, for the source of such a smile may be just as much the sublimity and subtlety of the truth as the folly of the ignorance that preceded it. As in the case of the smile of Kasyapa on the occasion of the Buddha's silently "preaching" the sandalwood flower, this is the smile of a fresh understanding which brings with it both release and reintegration at a profounder level. In Blyth's words, "laughter is a breaking through the intellectual barrier; at the moment of laughing something is understood; it needs no proof of itself."[23] Such an interpretation embraces both *anulara* and *anolarika*. Indeed, what finer source could laughter over foolishness have than a laughter from within the joy of some new-found, or re-found, insight?

It is out of such joy that even the most iconoclastic humor in Zen proceeds. Zen iconoclasm, for all its severity, conveys no animus or self-righteous indignation, but is grounded in the Bodhisattva ideal of enlightened compassion. However relentless its pursuit, or destructive its appearance, it is not motivated by dogmatism and intolerance, which would give it that arrogance and violence to which idol-smashing so easily falls prey. It is not an antagonistic humor with some hostile and aggressive intent, nor is it a self-enhancing strategy for reinforcing one's own position and action, but the humor of compassionate love (*karuna*) and affection (*metta*). If it laughs at ignorance and folly, if it debunks and ridicules and profanes, it does so out of the selfless wish to see others awakened and free.

There is, in fact, a certain lightness and liberty about this form of humor—sometimes giving it an air of frivolity and sacrilege, because it does not seem respectful enough. Yet such humor is not born of an inner compulsion to strike out at others in comic disguise, to fortify one's own persuasion by converting others to it, or to laugh those positions out of existence which threaten the position to which one is clinging. This is not the realm of anxiously attempting to prove something, to preach something, or protect something—of trying to "make something out of it." As Anagarika Govinda has phrased it: "The Buddha's sense of humor—which is so evident in many of his discourses—is closely bound up with his sense of compassion: both are born from an understanding of greater connections, from an insight into the interrelatedness of all things and all living beings and the chain reactions of cause and effect. His smile is the expression of one who can see the 'wondrous play of ignorance and knowledge' against its universal background and its deeper meaning. Only thus is it possible not to be overpowered by the misery of the world, or by our own sense of righteousness that judges and condemns what is not in accordance with our own understanding, and divides the world into good and bad. A man with a sense of humor cannot but be compassionate in his heart, because his sense of proportion allows him to see things in their proper perspective."[24]

In this context and spirit one may understand the unusual teaching of Master Ch'in-niu. Every day, it is reported, he would carry a cask of rice to the monks' quarters, crying out, "Dinner is ready, O Bodhisattvas!" and then bellow with laughter. For twenty years, according to the Zen records, he taught in this fashion. In the words of Hsueh-t'ou:

> *Enveloped in masses of white clouds,*
> *Peals of loud laughter we hear,*
> *Something is being delivered to us*
> *From both his hands. . .*[25]

To be sure, Hsueh-t'ou adds that his method involves a "deception," and that he was not "good-hearted." Yuan-wu, however, comments on this by saying, "Since Ch'in-niu descended into the weeds to help people, why did Hsueh-t'ou say that he wasn't good-hearted? Why did he talk this way? Patch-robed monks must have a living potential to begin to understand this."[26] In other words, Ch'in-niu, who laughingly called his monks Bodhisattvas, was the one behaving like a Bodhisattva ("descending into the weeds to help people"). Two puns were intended. Ch'in-niu's laughter was not just a laughter *at* his monks, even though it does contain an element of laughter at the ignorance, dullness, and self-centeredness of these budding Bodhi-sattvas. But this was also the compassionate, joyful, long-suffering laughter of one who has "gone beyond," who shows the way with a twinkle in the eyes, and who beckons all to follow—into that region where only Spirit reigns, and the Whole Truth may be told.

Both the use of words and not-using or abusing of words are properly expressions of compassion. The original preface to the compilation of *The Blue Cliff Records*—from which this case is taken—written by Pua-chao in 1128, says of the one hundred cases collected, along with commentary, verses, and word-play: "The ultimate path is in reality wordless; masters of our school extend compassion [by means of words and word-play] to rescue the fallen. If you see it like this, only then do you realize their thoroughgoing kindness. If, on the other hand, you get stuck on the phrases and sunk in the words, you won't avoid exterminating the Buddha's race."[27]

A touching instance of compassionate humor is given us in the story of the aged Roshi Yamamoto. At the age of ninety-six he was nearly blind, very feeble, and no longer able to teach or work in the monastery. He decided that he was only a burden to others, and that it was time for him to die. So he stopped eating. The younger monks, however, called to his attention the fact that it was not a convenient time for him to die, as it was January, and everyone would be uncomfortable at his funeral. Convinced by their reasoning that his death would be a burden to them, he agreed to resume eating. The monks were satisfied that they had won the argument, and that Yamamoto had abandoned the idea. But when it became warm again in the spring, the old master stopped eating, and died.[28]

CHAPTER TEN

The Child of Tao

Wise men hear and see
As little children do.
LAO-TZU

If you wish to write haiku
Find a three-foot child.
BASHO

Before the aged Nan-chu'an passed away, his head monk asked him, "Where are you going after your death?" The Master replied, "I am going down the hill to be a water buffalo." "Would it be possible to follow you there?" inquired the monk. Nan-chu'an responded, "If you want to follow me, please come with straw in your mouth!"[1]

At every level of its manifestation, humor spells freedom in some sense and to some degree. Humor means freedom. This is one of its most distinctive characteristics and virtues. Here, however, the freedom to laugh which moves within the conflicts and doubts and tensions of life—the freedom, therefore, which is still relative to bondage and ignorance—becomes the freedom to laugh on the other side (the inside) of enlightenment. To the extent that one is no longer in bondage to desire, or to the self, or the law, no longer torn apart by alienation and anxiety, no longer defined and determined primarily by seriousness, one can laugh with the laughter of little children and great sages. Humor is caught up, and brought to fulfillment, in the joy of awakening and emancipation.

A tiny bubble of laughter,
I am become the Sea of Mirth itself.[2]

Something of this spirit is captured in the account of the enlightenment of Shui-lao. When Shui-lao asked his master Ma-tsu a question,

Ma-tsu kicked him in the chest, knocking him to the ground. Immediately Shui-lao was awakened, got up, and began clapping his hands and laughing: "How marvellous! How marvellous! Hundreds of thousands of *samadhis* and innumerable spiritual insights have their root in the tip of a feather!" Later Shui-lao is reported to have said, "Since the master kicked me, I have not been able to stop laughing."[3] Humor at its highest and fullest is an expression of liberation and insight. It arises, not out of the illusions of *maya* or the ignorance of *avidya* or the graspings and clingings of *samsara*, but out of the awakenings of *bodhi* and *kensho*.

At the end of his life Lo-shan ascended the rostrum to speak. But instead of addressing his monks he abruptly dismissed them. He then remarked simply, "If you wish to show your gratitude for the Buddha's goodness to you, you should not be too earnest about propagating the Great Teaching," after which he began laughing loudly and died.[4] To see the world and one's individuality in this light is coincident with seeing it through the comic perspective, and in the comic spirit, at its profoundest level. It is as if a comic parenthesis had been placed around the whole of one's existence, and existence itself. To the degree that one is awakened, one is free to laugh in the deepest and most joyous sense, to laugh even in the face of the misfortunes of life and the inevitability of death.

> *Ever since my store-house burned*
> *I have had a clear view*
> *Of the risen moon.*
>
> Masahide

When Master P'u-hua sensed that his end was near, he announced to the people of the nearby town that he would go the next day to the Eastern Gate and die there. The whole community went in a procession behind him and assembled outside the city wall to pay their respects. P'u-hua then announced, "A funeral today would not be in accord with the blue crow [a mythological bird]. I will pass away tomorrow at the Southern Gate." The next day the people followed him again, but he announced, "It would be more auspicious to leave by the Western Gate tomorrow." On the third day fewer people came, and he decided on the North Gate instead. On the fourth day he picked up his own coffin and carried it out of the Northern Gate. Shaking his bell, he entered the coffin and passed away.[5]

The End is the New Beginning

In Zen, as in any religious context, there are three levels on which the comic moves in relation to the sacred, three moments or moods which in mythological terms may be seen as corresponding to the laughter of Paradise, Paradise-lost, and Paradise-regained. The use of such a mythological model is not arbitrary, nor simply a convenient methodological device. The various modes of the comic are well-symbolized by this mythical schema: the playful return to childish innocence and impulse, an iconoclastic and cathartic response to tensions and anxieties, and the recovery of childlikeness and freedom at a higher level. At all three levels is to be found, in one form or another, what Joseph Campbell has called, "the gift of immaturity itself, which has enabled us to retain in our best, most human, moments the capacity for play. . .It is, in fact, only those who have failed, one way or another [to preserve this gift] in their manhood or womanhood, who become our penny-dreadfuls, our gorillas and baboons."[6]

At the simplest level humor is a form of playing for the sake of playing. The clown cavorts, the comedian quips, the fool is foolish, and the spectator laughs out of sheer delight in the playfulness of the game of life itself. One is purposeless for the sake of being purposeless, nonsensical for the sake of being nonsensical, in a simple and innocent refusal to make sense, or to be orderly, or to "get serious" all the time. Here the comic spirit represents a leap into the playfulness of that "wild and careless, inexhaustible joy of life invincible."[7] It is not hostile or anxious or aggressive, but merely playful. It is the momentary, increasingly nostalgic, recapture of that world which is prior to the distinction between self and other, holy and unholy, cosmos and chaos, prior to the "knowledge of good and evil" and the emergence of shame and guilt. It is, in short, the world that is symbolized by the mythical picture of a primeval Paradise, the "Urzeit" that in Zen comes to be projected onto a higher plane as the "Endzeit" of human experience.

160

Humor is not all innocence and play, however. At a more sophisticated and self-conscious level it stands more immediately within the sphere of duality, and in sensitivity to its conflicts and tensions, its alienations and anxieties. Here it is not a humor which leaves behind the world of dichotomy and contradiction in a holiday of innocent abandon—a marvellously whimsical yet inherently unstable interlude—but is a humor which moves within the terms and delineations of the objectified self in comic response to them. It is, consequently, the comic mood as it corresponds to the fallen state of Paradise-lost: the state of self-assertion, of desiring and grasping, of separation and estrangement. This form of humor is more self-conscious, more reflective, more serious. In fact, it shares in the same dualistic rifts in experience which elicit it and to which it is an inverted response. One senses a preliminary attempt at raising the matter to a higher plane by seeing the foolishness and humor in the situation, and placing things in larger perspective. But the tendency is to be satisfied with a momentary release of tension and conflict. Humor, at this level, does not quite get off the ground. It is not liberating, but only cathartic. Nevertheless, in the freedom of this capacity to stand apart from the situation and see some comedy in it lies the saving potentiality of humor. The clown's ability to garble distinctions, and the fool's inability to make the proper distinctions, prevision the sage's capacity for moving beyond discrimination and duality.

To the degree that such insight and liberation takes place, it becomes possible to speak of a third level of humor. Here humor becomes the freedom to laugh and play which is contained within the freedom of enlightenment. The playfulness and laughter of childlike spontaneity and naturalness has been recaptured on a profounder level, a level corresponding mythically to Paradise-regained. One has now become free, in the deepest and fullest sense, to laugh.

Beyond Good and Evil

In Taoism—undoubtedly influencing the early Ch'an masters—the schematization of this achievement is that of seeing the form of the child as the model for the form of the sage. The sage does not return to childhood, *per se*, as if the sentimentality or senility of a second childhood were being recommended, but recovers as a sage the lost characteristics of childhood: purity, simplicity, unity, innocence, immediacy, spontaneity, naturalness, freedom.

For classical Taoism the principal ethical and religious question is that posed by Lao-tzu: "Have you reached the state of a new-born babe?" The paradigm of a full humanity is to be found in the effortless and unitary spontaneity of the child, which is the nature of the Tao itself. To "return again to infancy" is to "return again to Primal, Simplicity." This is to be a true child of Tao. The sage, therefore, is one who "desires to be desireless," having the "virtue of non-striving." Thus, while "all the people strain their ears and eyes, the sage only smiles like an amused infant."[8] As Chuang-tzu rephrases Lao-tzu's position:

> *Can you be like an infant*
> *That cries all day*
> *Without getting a sore throat.*
> *Or clenches his fist all day*
> *Without getting a sore hand,*
> *Or gazes all day*
> *Without eyestrain?*
> *You want the first elements?*
> *The infant has them.*
> *Free from care, unaware of self,*
> *He acts without reflection.*[9]

This is not, however, simply a regression to infancy, as the passage seems to imply. When a disciple asks, "Is this perfection?" Chuang-tzu has Lao-tzu respond:

> *Not at all.*
> *It is only the beginning;*
> *This melts the ice.*
> *This enables you to unlearn*
> *So that you can be led by Tao,*
> *Be a child of Tao.*[10]

According to Chuang-tzu, the Taoist master Nu-yu was once asked, "Sir, you are advanced in years, and yet you still have the face of a child. What can be the secret?'' Said Nu-yu, ''I have been instructed in the Tao.''[11] To have drunk deeply of Tao, to have become a true child of Tao, is to have discovered, as it were, the fountain of eternal youth. This, in the teaching of the Sixth Patriarch, is a recovery of the Tao of one's ''original nature,'' which is not to be understood as a return to a thoughtless state. For such would render one ''equivalent to insentient beings, and would be a cause of hindrance in the Way.'' Rather, it is an achievement of attachment-less thought, for ''non-attachment is man's original nature'' and ''that is freedom.''[12]

On this plane of non-attachment, the humor of the sage becomes the humor of an acceptance and celebration of the thusness and suchness of the world, transcending the anxiety over possessing and not-possessing, existing and not-existing, success and failure, the unrecoverable past and the unattainable future. The sage does not attempt to live in the abstract world of the desiring self, habitually refusing the reality of the immediate moment in favor of some bygone moment or anticipated moment or ideal moment—which would be a failure to really live at all. For the past, by definition, no longer exists; the future, as future, can never come; and the ideal, if actualized, could not be the ideal as such. The sage is one who, in the freedom of non-attachment and the immediacy of the present, is able to accept life and laugh at life, to receive life and live life, in ''good humor'' in spite of its tensions and contradictions. Such a one has entered in Yuan-wu's terms, ''the *ksana'* instant in which 'ordinary' and 'holy' are transcended.''[13]

Though there is an apparent danger that this good-humored acceptance and celebration of life may sever the nerve of moral action and intellectual vision, it nevertheless represents a plane of transcendence apart from which one is hopelessly embroiled in the ultra-seriousness of an insatiable striving, and in the futility of constantly emptying the present moment in favor of the unreality of past or future or ideal moments.

In the words attributed to the Sixth Patriarch: ''For him who has once had an insight into his own Nature, no special posture as a form of meditation is to be recommended. Everything and anything is good to him, sitting, or lying, or standing. He enjoys perfect freedom of

163

spirit, he moves along as he feels, and yet he does nothing wrong. He is always acting in accord with his Self-Nature. His work is play." [14] Lin-chi, likewise, counsels his disciples: "Followers of Tao, the way of Buddhism admits of no artificial effort. It only consists in doing the ordinary things without any fuss: going to the stool, making water, putting on clothes, taking a meal, sleeping when tired. Let the fools laugh at me. Only the wise know what I mean. . .The truly noble man is a man of no concern and no ado. Don't try to be clever and ingenious. Just be ordinary." [15]

The freedom from self and law is suggested in the story about Tanzan (1819-92), who was noted, among other things, for his lack of scrupulousness in keeping the Buddha's precepts with respect to sleeping, eating, drinking, etc. Though frequently looked upon with suspicion by those who had not gone very far beyond the level of "washing the cup on the outside," Tanzan nevertheless persisted in his freedom from bondage to the law. One of the Buddha's precepts, of course, has to do with the monks' relations to women. On one occasion Tanzan was travelling with another monk, Ekido, down a muddy road, where they met a beautiful girl in a fine silk kimono, unable to cross the intersection. Lifting her in his arms, Tanzan carried her across the road. Ekido did not speak to Tanzan until they reached a lodging temple that night, when he finally exploded angrily: "Monks do not go near females, especially young and lovely ones!" "I left the girl there at the crossroads," replied Tanzan simply. "Are you still carrying her?" [16]

Unfortunately, this freedom is sometimes confused with a shallow imitation of certain of the more bizarre, profane, or incidental expressions of some of the great Zen masters, thus setting up a new orthodoxy of unorthodoxies—as if to behave strangely, or look peculiar, or become immoral or anti-intellectual is somehow a sign of authentic Zen and proof of spiritual maturity. It is like Lin-chi's monks who expended so much effort in imitating the master's renowned shouting that Lin-chi forbade any further shouting in the monastery until his disciples could first demonstrate their understanding of the meaning and proper moment for the shout, and even then not unless it became a natural and authentic expression of their own person and situation. Yun-men was not so charitable about it: "If you meet an old monk raising a finger or a dust-whisk [imitating the manner of certain masters] and saying, 'This is Ch'an, this is Tao,' you should raise your staff, give him a blow, break his head and then leave the place!''[17] But then Chu-ti was even less circumspect, summarily cutting off the finger of the attendant who copied his "one finger Zen" without having the corresponding spiritual attainment, leaving him with a "no-finger" Zen!

The assumption seems to be that if one simulates certain of the incidental, or even substantive, consequences of enlightenment one becomes enlightened—which is like the man who leaps into the sea with the carefree abandon of the experienced swimmer, but who has not first learned how to swim. He drowns in his own pretensions! Greater than the problem of mimicry, however, is the confusion of spiritual freedom and spontaneity with a justification for some of the crassest forms of license which, under the guise of liberation, become but another convenient excuse for doing as one pleases. Still less is this freedom in Zen to be confounded with giving free reign to certain infantile or animal impulses, and therefore presumably to the most "natural" instincts. The problem is not one of the inhibition and repression of various elemental drives which must be released in order for the individual to be liberated. This would be a relapse of the lowest sort. Instead of making an advance on the situation, this confuses impulsiveness for immediacy, indulgence for naturalness, and insensitivity for innocence. Under the mask of spirituality it is little more than a grand rationalization for a retreat to some of the basest forms of ego, ignorance, and desire. Like nudists who may imagine themselves emancipated, but who have only become unbuttoned, such a misinterpretation of Zen freedom has mistaken a return to the irresponsible spontaneity of the child for a genuinely mature form of spontaneousness. Child*likeness* is not to be equated with child*ishness*. The spiritual goal is not a giant step backward into a personal or primordial infancy, but the regeneration of one's Original Nature.

It is not that there is something so wrong about childhood, or in recovering moments of childish playfulness, as if one should forever be cut off from those moments which were once one's beginning and one's very life, or as if childhood were something to be despised.

This is hardly the spirit which Pu-tai, spurning monastic life and playing and dancing and laughing with village children, symbolizes. The adult who has forgotten what it means to be a child, who gives little evidence of ever having been a child, who is completely out of touch with this former self, is hardly the wiser or richer for it—aged, perhaps, but not matured. In fact, for all the solemnity in such seriousness and no-nonsense, and for all the air of dignity and importance, one may be further from spiritual maturity than the child which is held in contempt. From this standpoint, most of what passes for adulthood (spiritual or otherwise) is really only an extension of adolescence. It is none other than a continuation of the adolescent attempt at demonstrating maturity by proving that one is no longer a child. The adolescent imagines that adulthood is achieved simply through a process of forgetting, repudiating, and ultimately negating childhood. Not yet discovered is the fact that maturity is only reached by becoming once again like a little child.

The achievement of the comic spirit and perspective at its fullest in Zen may be interpreted as a corollary of the recovery on a higher level of that spontaneity, immediacy, and naturalness enjoyed by the child—the freedom that is prior to the emergence of rationality and order, and the hiatus in experience between self and world, mind and body, good and evil, sacred and profane. Humor in Zen, therefore, at its profoundest is a humor that transcends all those categories with which we would coerce the world, and which in turn make us captives in our own prison. It has risen above both the ignorance that is innocence, and the ignorance that offers a knowledge of good and evil. It is the playfulness and lightheartedness that lies beyond our restless grasping and clinging, beyond the eternal torment of Tantalus, the sense of gaiety and festivity that lies on the further side of fear of death and attachment to the forms of life. One has learned what it means to become a child again, in the wisdom of the sage, the child of Tao.

The Laughter of Paradise-Regained

Most interpretations of humor recognize its existence on only two levels, corresponding mythically to the laughter of Paradise and

Paradise-lost. It is no doubt correct that most expressions of humor are instances of one or the other of these two types. Freud, for example, saw humor as essentially the endeavor to regain "a pleasure which has really been lost in the development of (psychic) activity. For the euphoria which we are thus striving to obtain is nothing but the state of a bygone time, in which we were wont to defray our psychic work with slight expenditure. It is the state of our childhood in which we did not know the comic, were incapable of wit, and did not need humor to make us happy."[18] This thesis gives to humor essentially a nostalgic moment of regression to the paradise of infancy, along with the function of giving vent to impulses of hostility, aggression, and desire which have been repressed and held in check by social restriction and inhibition. What it fails to recognize is the possibility of a recovery of childlikeness on a higher plane of being and knowing. In his *Iron Flute Blown Upside Down* Genro captures this movement with characteristic wit:

> *The bellows blew high the flaming forge;*
> *The sword was hammered on the anvil.*
> *It was the same steel as in the beginning,*
> *But how different was its edge!*[19]

Erich Fromm has argued: "Basically, there can only be two answers. One is to overcome separateness and find unity by *regression* to the state of unity which existed before awareness ever arose, that is, before man was born. The other answer is to be *fully born,* to develop one's awareness, one's reason, one's capacity to love, to such a point that one transcends one's own egocentric involvement, and arrives at a new harmony, at a new oneness with the world."[20] The humor which corresponds to this level is not reducible to the laughter of the child, nor to that of the adolescent. It is the laughter of maturity, the laughter of the *fully born,* to use Fromm's felicitous phrase.

Here there is no restless, anxious, striving humor driven by the dramatic tensions of life, but an effortless, tranquil humor: the humor of *wu wei,* of harmonious rather than tense activity. Its motivating force is not nervousness and insecurity, seeking self-reinforcement and easily given to belligerence. Rather it is the humor of inner

167

stability and serenity, which therefore is capable of becoming, in the purest sense, the humor of compassion.

This is clearly the most dynamic and self-contained form of humor. For it does not derive its impulse from tension and anxiety, and therefore in large part from an outside source in relation to which it is dependent and determined—however well it may function as a mechanism for releasing pent-up energies, ameliorating conflicts, or redirecting animosities into less violent channels. It does not proceed out of a position of weakness, but of strength. Its power arises from an inner harmony and assurance, and thus it moves with a force that flows from unity rather than opposition and strife. Grounded in *wu-shih* (no concern) and *wu-ch'in* (no seeking), this is the laughter of the highest freedom: freedom from all oppression of self and other, of desire and attachment, or of meaning and meaninglessness. Whether expressed in the serene smile of *sita* or the raucous laughter of *apahasita* and *atihasita*, such humor lies beyond both seriousness and frivolity, sense and nonsense, purpose and purposelessness, in that joy which, as Chuang-tzu says, "does all things without concern."[21]

In this achievement is the solution to the touching nostalgia for the irretrievable paradise of Wordsworth's "Recollections of Early Childhood":

> *Heaven lies about us in our infancy!*
> *Shades of the prison-house begin to close*
> *Upon the growing Boy. . .*
> *At length the Man perceives it die away,*
> *And fade into the light of common day.*

The world ruled by seriousness alone grows old, gnarled, sterile, wooden, rigid, lifeless. The grave world, indeed, is the world of the grave. But the world in the reign of the comic spirit grows young again—lively, vital, creative, dancing, joyful. It is a world that is not guarded, like Eden, by an angel with a flaming sword, but by Pu-tai and Ryokan, Han-shan and Shih-te, and the laughing sages of Hu-hsi.

Three metamorphoses of the spirit do I designate to you:
how the spirit becomes a camel, the camel a lion, and the

lion at last a child.

Many heavy things are there for the spirit, the strong load-bearing spirit in which reverence dwells; for the heavy and the heaviest longs its strength . . . All these heaviest things the load-bearing spirit takes upon itself; and like the camel which, when laden, hastens into the wilderness, so hastens the spirit into its wilderness.

But in the loneliest wilderness happens the second metamorphosis: here the spirit becomes a lion. Freedom will it capture, and lordship in its own wilderness. Its last Lord it here seeks; hostile will it be to him, and to its last God. For victory will it struggle with the great dragon.

But tell me, my brethren, what the child can do, which even the lion could not do? Why has the preying lion still to become a child? Innocence is the child, and forgetfulness, a new beginning, a game, a self-rolling wheel, a first movement, a holy Yea.

Nietzsche, *Thus Spake Zarathustra*[22]

Epilogue

A contemporary Ch'an master, Hsuan Hua, thus concluded his talk at the end of a *sesshin*, or week of intensive meditation:

> Now we have finished. Everyone stand and we will bow to the Buddha three times to thank him. We thank him, because even if we did not have a great enlightenment, we had a small enlightenment. If we did not have a small enlightenment, at least we didn't get sick. If we got sick, at least we didn't die. So let's thank the Buddha.[1]

Notes

Chapter I: The Other Side of Zen

1. R.H. Blyth, *Zen and Zen Classics*, 7 volumes (Tokyo: Hokuseido, 1960-70), V, page 198.
2. Harold G. Henderson, *An Introduction to Haiku* (Garden City: Doubleday, 1958), page 169.
3. John C.H. Wu, *The Golden Age of Zen* (Taipei: National War College, 1967), page 145.
4. Chiang Yee, *The Chinese Eye*, 2nd edition (London: Norton, 1936), page 81.
6. Shwe Zan Aung, *The Compendium of Philosophy: A Translation of the Abhidhammatha-Sanghaha*, rev. and ed. by Mrs. Rhys Davids (London: Luzac, 1910), pages 25-6.
7. Bartholomaeus Anglicus, *De proprietatibus rerum* 5.41.61.
8. Nyogen Senzaki and Ruth S. McCandless, trans. with commentary of Genro's "Solid Iron Flute," *The Iron Flute* (Rutland: Tuttle, 1961), page 126.
9. Sohaku Ogata, trans., *The Transmission of the Lamp: Early Masters* (Wolfeboro, NH: Longwood Academic, 1989). X.5.1 (References for the Longwood edition are to book, person, and episode).
10. Heinrich Dumoulin, *A History of Zen Buddhism* (New York: Random House, 1963), page 100.
11. Ogata, *Transmission* IV.11.4.
12. "The Dragon's Song" given here and the opening inscriptions for chapters 3, 4, 6, 7, and 8 are from *The Transmission of the Lamp*, from which selections are translated by Chang Chung-yuan, *Original Teachings of Ch'an Buddhism* (New York: Pantheon, 1969), pages 78, 169, 141, 143 and 95, 69, 104, 203 respectively.

Chapter II: The Smile of Truth

1. Henderson, page 147.
2. R.H. Blyth, *Haiku*, 4 volumes (Tokyo: Hokuseido, 1949-52), IV, 49.
3. Henderson, page 142.
4. *Wu-men-kuan (Mumonkan*, 1229 CE), trans. Sohaku Ogata, *Zen for the West* (London: Rider, 1959), pages 97-8.

5. Charles Luk, *Ch'an and Zen Teaching*, 3 volumes (London: Rider, 1960-2), I, 131.
6. Suzuki, *Sengai the Zen Master*, (London: Faber and Faber, 1971), page 147.
7. Blyth, *Oriental Humour*, (Tokyo: Hokuseida Press, 1959), page 87.
8. Ogata, *Transmission* VIII.39.4.
9. *Ibid.*, II.6.1.
10. *Ibid.*, IX.1.7.
11. *Ibid.*, IX.3.3.
12. Bharata, *Natya Shastra*, VI, vv. 61-2. Cf. Shwe Zan Aung, *The Compendium of Philosophy*, pages 22-5.
13. Shwe Zan Aung, *Compendium*, page 26.
14. *The Middle Way*, XLV (August, 1970), page 91.
15. Blyth, *Oriental Humour*, page 331.
16. Suzuki, *Sengai*, page 10.
17. *Ibid.*, page 134.

Chapter III: Zen Masters and Clown Figures

1. *Pi-yen-lu (Hekigan-roku)*, case 68. R.D.M. Shaw, translator and editor, *The Blue Cliff Records* (London: Michael Joseph, 1961), page 212.
2. Luk, I, 144.
3. Ogata, *Transmission* VII.10.4.
4. Paul Reps and Nyogen Senzaki, *Zen Flesh, Zen Bones: A Collection of Zen and Pre-Zen Writings* (Garden City, Doubleday, 1959), pages 60-1.
5. E.O. Reischauer, translator and editor, *Ennin's Diary* (New York: Ronald, 1955), page 210. This comment is made with reference to twenty Ch'an monks whom he met at a Ch'an monastery.
6. *My Country and My People* (New York: Reynal, 1935), page 52 ff.
7. G.P. Fedotov, *The Russian Religious Mind*, 2 volumes (Cambridge: Harvard University Press, 1966), II, 316-43.
8. Blyth, *Zen Classics*, II, 47.
9. D.T. Suzuki, *Essays in Zen Buddhism*, 3 series (London: Rider, 1949-53), III, 46.
10. *Wu-men-kuan*, case 3.
11. Isshu Miura and Ruth Fuller Sasaki, *Zen Dust: The History of the Koan and Koan Study in Rinzai (Lin-chi) Zen* (New York: Harcourt, Brace and World, 1966), pages 82-3.
12. Wu, page 101.
13. Blyth, *Zen Classics*, II, 11.

14. Ogata, *Transmission* VI.1.1.
15. D.T. Suzuki, *Zen and Japanese Culture* (New York: Pantheon, 1959), page 365.
16. Miura and Sasaki, pages 124-5.
17. Suzuki, *Japanese Culture*, plate 40.
18. Blyth, *Oriental Humour*, pages 93-4.
19. Enid Welsford, *The Fool: His Social and Literary History* (London: Faber, 1935), page 319.
20. *Ibid.*, page 321.
21. Lucien Stryk and Takashi Ikemoto, *Zen: Poems, Prayers, Sermons, Anecdotes and Interviews* (Garden City: Doubleday, 1963), page 98.
22. Ogata, *Transmission* X.4.39.
23. Suzuki, III, 145.
24. Hugo Munsterberg, *Zen and Oriental Art* (Rutland: Tuttle, 1965), page 34.
25. Henri L. Jolly, *Legend and Japanese Art* (Rutland: Tuttle, 1967), pages 120-2.
26. Munsterberg, page 55.
27. Reps and Senzaki, page 16.
28. Luk, I, 111.
29. Arthur Waley, *An Introduction to the Study of Chinese Painting* (New York: Scribners, 1923), pages 228-9.
30. George Rowley, *Principles of Chinese Painting*, 2nd edition (Princeton: Princeton University Press, 1959), page 17.
31. *Ibid.*, page 14.
32. Waley, page 48.
33. *T'ang-ch'ao-ming-hua-lu*, translated by Alexander C. Soper, *Archives of the Chinese Art Society of America*, IV (1950), page 20.
34. Cited in Chang Yen-yuan's *Li-tai-ming-hua-chi* (AD 847). W.R.B. Acker, *Some T'ang and Pre-T'ang Texts on Chinese Painting* (Leiden: E.J. Brill, 1954).
35. S. Shimada, "Concerning the I-P'in Style of Painting, Part I," translated by J. Cahill, *Oriental Art*, VII (Summer, 1961), page 69.
36. *Ibid.*, pages 68-9.
37. Alexander C. Soper, translator, *Kuo Jo-Hsu's Experiences in Painting* (Washington. American Council of Learned Societies, 1951), page 44.
38. *Ibid.*, page 61.
39. *Ibid.*, page 81.
40. *Ibid.*, pages 28-9.
41. Lin Yutang, *The Chinese Theory of Art* (New York: Putnam, 1967), page 98.
42. Yee, page 158.
43. Soper, *Kuo Jo-Hsu*, page 8.

44. Osvald Siren, *Chinese Painting, Leading Masters and Principles,* 7 volumes (New York: Ronald, 1956-8), II, 11.
45. Munsterberg, page 53.
46. Siren, II, 138.
47. Siren, I, 161.
48. *Ibid.,* pages 163-4.
49. Wu, page 144.
50. D.T. Suzuki, *The Zen Doctrine of No-Mind* (London: Rider, 1949), page 86.
51. Welsford, pages 324-6.

Chapter IV: Laughing at the Buddhas and Abusing the Patriarchs

1. *Pi-yen-lu,* case 4; Shaw, pages 34-5.
2. Suzuki, *Essays* I, 188-9.
3. Ogata, *Transmission* VIII.3.35.
4. *Ibid.,* X.20.1.
5. *Ibid.,* VIII.3.4.
6. Suzuki, I, 330.
7. Hu Shih, "Ch'an (Zen) Buddhism in China," *Philosophy East and West,* III (April, 1953), page 22.
8. Wu, page 138.
9. *Ibid.,* page 211.
10. *Ibid.,* pages 196-7.
11. Luk, II, 114.
12. Suzuki, III, 373.
13. Shaw, page 32, n. 4.
14. Suzuki, II, 146.
15. *Ibid.,* page 55 n. 3.
16. M. Anesaki, *Buddhist Art in Relation to Buddhist Ideals* (Boston: Houghton Mifflin, 1923), page 28.
17. Blyth, *Oriental Humour,* page 266.
18. Blyth, *Zen Classics,* V, 188.
19. Ogata, *Transmission* I.7.3.
20. Luk, II, 208.
21. Ogata, *Transmission* IX.1.11.
22. Suzuki, III, 69.
23. *Ibid.,* page 58.
24. Suzuki, II, 85.
25. Wu, page 250.

26. John Blofeld, translator, *The Zen Teaching of Hui Hai* (London: Rider, 1962), page 123.
27. Thomas Merton, *The Way of Chuang-Tzu* (New York: New Directions, 1965), xxvi, II.
28. Luk, II, 121.
29. Ogata, *Zen for the West*, page 85.
30. Blyth, *Zen Classics*, IV, 321.
31. *Revelation* 22:18, 19 (RSV).
32. Reps and Senzaki, page 65.
33. Wu, page 92.
34. Suzuki, I, 176.
35. *Wu-men-kuan*, case 6; Ogata, pages 98-9.
36. *Ibid.*, case 41, page 125.
37. Jolly, pages 120-2.
38. Blyth, *Oriental Humour*, page 414.
39. Suzuki, II, 27.
40. *The Way of the White Clouds* (London: Hutchinson, 1956), page 176.
41. *Ibid.*, pages 176-7.

Chapter V: The Buddha and the Bullfrog

1. George Santayana, *The Sense of Beauty* (New York: Scribners, 1896), page 188.
2. Kenji Toda, *Japanese Scroll Paintings* (Chicago: University of Chicago Press, 1935), pages 53 ff.
3. Similarly in 1916, when two statues in the Toshodaiji temple were removed for repairs, playful sketches were discovered on the stands underneath. Dating from the 8th century, they included a motley array of not-particularly-divine figures: horses, monkeys, birds, rabbits, frogs and a mantis. *Ibid.*, pages 49-50.
4. Siren, IV, 11.
5. Brief descriptions of the wall paintings found in Buddhist temples and monasteries in China prior to the destruction of many of them in 845-9 are to be found in the *Li-tai-ming-hua-chi*. Cf. Acker, pages 254-377.
6. See T. Naito, *The Wall Paintings of Horyuji*, translated by W.R.B. Acker and B. Rowland (Baltimore: Waverly, 1943).
7. D.T. Suzuki, *Zen and Japanese Buddhism*, 4th edition (Tokyo: Japanese Tourist Bureau, 1965), p. 35.
8. *Essays in the Philosophy of Art* (Bloomington: Indiana University Press, 1946), pages 81-2.
9. Cf. Helen B. Chapin, "Three Early Portraits of Bodhidharma," *Archives of the Chinese Society of America*, I (1945-6), pages 66-97.

10. Suzuki, *Japanese Culture,* page 379.
11. Charles Luk, *Secrets of Chinese Meditation* (London: Rider, 1964), pages 94-5.
12. Suzuki, III, 82.
13. Siren, V, 69.
14. Suzuki, III, 107.
15. Naito, pages 59 ff.
16. Suzuki, III, 372.
17. Cf. Suzuki, *Japanese Culture,* page 348.
18. Osvald Siren, *The Chinese and the Art of Painting* (Peiping, 1936), page 91.
19. Munsterberg, page 90.
20. Hu Shih, "The Development of Zen Buddhism in China," *The Chinese Social and Political Science Review,* XV (April, 1932), pages 481-2.
21. Ogata, *Transmission* II.13.2.
22. Merton, page 16.
23. Yutang, *My People,* page 89.
24. From the *Hsuan-ho-hua-p'u* (1120) and the *Li-tai-ming-hua-chi* (847).
25. Teng-chu'un's *Hua-chi* (1167) seems to suggest a Ch'an monk, while in the *Hsuan-ho-hua-p'u* this advice was given by a Taoist.
26. Cf. Agnes Meyer, *Chinese Painting, as Reflected in the Thought and Art of Li Lung-mien* (New York: Duffield, 1923), pages 56-8.
27. Siren, II, 55.
28. Ogata, *Transmission* X.1.14.
29. Luk, II, 74.
30. Wu, page 89.
31. *Ibid.,* page 230.
32. Suzuki, *Japanese Culture,* page 248.
33. Blyth, *Haiku,* II, 235.
34. Henderson, pages 18, 53.
35. Luk, *Secrets,* pages 95-6.
36. Wu, page 247.
37. Luk, II, 191.
38. Wu, page 182.
39. Nancy Wilson Ross, editor, *The World of Zen* (New York: Random House, 1960), page 123.
40. No author, *Zen Buddhism* (Mt. Vernon: Peter Pauper, 1959), page 33.
41. Suzuki, III, 78-95.

1. Siren, II, 132.
2. Suzuki, III, 89.
3. Wu, page 250.
4. Suzuki, III, 77-8.
5. Grock, *Life's a Lark* (New York: Benjamin Bloom, 1969), pages 17 and 52.
6. Wu, page 247.
7. Ogata, *Transmission* IV.10.3.
8. Luk, II, 193.
9. *Pi-yen-lu,* case 95; Shaw, page 276.
10. Luk, II, 188.
11. Suzuki, III, 368-9.
12. Reps and Senzaki, page 68.
13. Garma C.C. Chang, *The Practice of Zen* (New York: Harper, 1959).
14. Wu, page 266.
15. Luk, II, 187.
16. *Ibid.,* page 35.
17. Suzuki, III, 87, translates this: "How wondrously supernatural, and how miraculous this! I draw water, and I carry fuel!"
18. Suzuki, *No-Mind,* page 104.
19. Blyth, *Oriental Humour,* page 91.
20. Suzuki, I, 257.
21. Philip Kapleau, *The Wheel of Death* (New York: Harper and Row, 1971), page 67.
22. John Blofeld, translator, *The Zen Teaching of Huang Po* (New York: Grove, 1959), page 29.
23. Wu, page 40.
24. Blyth, *Oriental Humour,* page 89.
25. Suzuki, III, 59.
26. Henderson, pages 58, 151.
27. Suzuki, II, 249.
28. George Santayana, *Soliloquies in England and Later Soliloquies* (New York: Scribners, 1922), pages 141-2.
29. Ogata, *Transmission* VI.8.2.
30. *Ibid.,* VII.15.5.
31. *An Essay on Laughter* (London: Longmans, 1902), page 384.
32. Henderson, page 153.
33. Gerardus van der Leeuw, *Religion in Essence and Manifestation,* translated by J.E. Turner (New York: Harper, 1963), II, page 680.
34. Suzuki, III, 319

35. *Ibid.,* page 348.
36. Suzuki, *Japanese Culture,* page 262.
37. Johan Huizinga, *Homo Ludens* (Boston: Beacon, 1950), page 119.

Chapter VII: The Folly of the Desiring Self

1. *The Journey to the West,* Vol. 1, translated and edited by Anthony C. Yu (Chicago: University of Chicago Press, 1977).
2. Ogata, *Transmission* V.7.1.
3. William Willeford, *The Fool and His Scepter* (Evanston: Northwestern University Press, 1969), pages 33-9.
4. Ogata, *Transmission* V.19.15.
5. Reps and Senzaki, pages 31-2.
6. Irmgard Schoegl, *The Wisdom of the Zen Masters,* 1976), page 47.
7. "Utterance', *Festival* (New York: Braziller, 1966), page 82.
8. Suzuki, II, 33.
9. *Senkai-ichiran* (Tokyo, 1958), pages 71-2.
10. Luk, II, 199.
11. *Open Secret* (Hong Kong: Hong Kong University Press, 1965), page 167.
12. Philip Yampolsky, *The Zen Master Hakuin: Selected Writings* (New York: Columbia University Press, 1971), pages 118-19.
13. Irving Babbit, translator, *The Dhammapada* (New York: New Directions, 1965), v. 62-3, 66.
14. Merton, xxiii, 8.
15. Luk, II, 171-2.
16. *Thoughts on Jesting* (1764), edited by Joseph Jones (Austin: University of Texas Press, 1947), pages 55-6.
17. Luk, II, 95.
18. Suzuki, III, 36-7.
19. Blyth, *Zen Classics,* V, 175.
20. Luk, II, 185 n. 2.
21. "Sengai: Zen and Art," *Art News Annual,* 56 (November, 1957), page 196.
22. Hermann Hesse, *Steppenwolf* (New York: Holt, Rinehart and Winston, 1963), page 111.
23. The *Chuang-tzu,* 32.9. My translation.
24. Ogata, *Transmission* IX.1.15.
25. Welsford, page 37.
26. *Anatomy of Criticism,* (Princeton: Princeton University Press, 1957), pages 163-86.

27. Merton, xii, I.
28. Suzuki, II, 100.
29. *Varieties of Religious Experience* (New York: Longmans, Green, 1902), chapters 4-8. See Conrad Hyers, *Once-Born, Twice-Born Zen: The Soto and Rinzai Schools of Japan* (Wolfeboro, NH: Longwood Academic, 1989).
30. *Buddhism* (London: Penguin Books, 1951), page 184.
31. *The Way of Zen* (New York: Pantheon, 1957), page 155.
32. Suzuki, III, 30.
33. *Ibid.*, page 35.
34. Max Muller, translator, *Anecdota Oxoniensia*, I, I (1881), page 27.
35. Dumoulin, page 164.
36. Suzuki, III, 54.
37. Luk, II, 114.
38. Suzuki, III, 54.
39. *Ibid.*, page 45.
40. Ogata, *Transmission* IV.1.4.
41. Wu, page 215.
42. *Wu-men-kuan*, case 41; Ogata, *Zen for the West*, page 125.
43. Ogata, *Transmission* III.2.2.

Chapter VIII: Socrates in China

1. D.T. Suzuki, *Studies in the Lankavatara Sutra* (London: Routledge, 1930), page 107.
2. N.a., *Zen Buddhism*, page 17. Cf. Luk, I, 136-7.
3. Ogata, *Transmission* VI.2.1.
4. Suzuki, II, 48.
5. Wu, page 84.
6. Luk, I, 129.
7. Wu, page 146.
8. *Tai-hui-pu-shuo*, compiled by T'su-ching (1190).
9. Cited in Paramahansa Yogananda, *Autobiography of a Yogi* (Rider, 1969), page 349 n.
10. Ogata, *Transmission* V.19.8.
11. Luk, II, 189-90.
12. *Ibid.*, page 205.
13. Dwight Goddard, translator, *Self-Realization of Noble Wisdom* (Thetford, Vt.: Private printing, 1932), page 78.
14. Ogata, *Transmission* IV.16.2.
15. *Ibid.*, IV.1.1.

179

16. Wu, page 188.
17. Suzuki, III, 43.
18. Wu, page 16.
19. Suzuki, II, 33.
20. Merton, xii, 10.
21. My translation.
22. Ogata, *Transmission* IX.22.1.
23. Soren Kierkegaard, *Philosophical Fragments*, translated by David F. Swenson (Princeton: Princeton University Press, 1936), page 7.
24. Ogata, *Transmission* IV.12.4.
25. This tale was related to me by Lama Anagarika Govinda.
26. Wm. Theodore de Bary, et al., *Sources of the Chinese Tradition* (New York: Columbia University Press, 1960), page 404.
27. Suzuki, *No-Mind*, page 92.
28. Wu, page 233.
29. *Ibid.*, page 137.
30. Blyth, *Zen Classics*, II, 58.
31. Senzaki and McCandless, page 129.
32. E.R. Hughes, "Epistemological Methods in Chinese Philosophy," *The Chinese Mind*, edited by Charles A. Moore (Honolulu: East-West Center Press, 1967), page 78.
33. Blyth, *Oriental Humour*, page 90.
34. Blyth, *Zen Classics*, II, 122.
35. Luk, II, 194.
36. Wu, page 152.
37. Ogata, *Transmission* IV.10.2.
38. Francis H. Cook, *Sounds of Valley Streams* (Albany: State University of New York Press, 1989), p. 78.
39. *Ibid.*, page 80.

Chapter IX: Getting the Point of the Joke

1. Luk, I, 11.
2. Luk, II, 58.
3. *Wu-men-kuan*, case 19; Ogata, *Zen for the West*, page 108.
4. Suzuki, III, 105.
5. Goddard, page 70.
6. Suzuki, II, 223.
7. *Wu-men-kuan*, case 18.
8. Ogata, *Transmission* X.4.30.
9. *Ibid.*, VIII.3.16.
10. Suzuki, II, 89.

11. Senzaki and McCandless, translators, *The Iron Flute*.
12. Blyth, *Zen Classics*, V, 197.
13. A common Buddhist simile, and the title of a collection of Zen texts in 10 volumes, *Shigetsuroku*, 1602.
14. *Wu-men-kuan*, case 3.
15. Goddard, page 46.
16. Luk, I, 10.
17. Luk, II, 191.
18. Luk, I, 129.
19. Suzuki, II, 97.
20. *Ibid.*, page 252.
21. Blyth, *Oriental Humour*, page 89.
22. Shwe Zan Aung, *Compendium*, pages 23-4.
23. Blyth, *Oriental Humour*, page 91.
24. Govinda, page 177.
25. Suzuki, *Sengai*, page 9.
26. Thomas and J.C. Cleary, *The Blue Cliff Records*, Vol. III (Boulder, Colorado: Shambala, 1977), page 490.
27. *Ibid.*, page vii.
28. Kapleau, *Wheel of Death*, page 67.

Chapter X: The Child of Tao

1. Chung-yuan, *Original Teachings of Ch'an Buddhism*, page 163.
2. "Samadhi," Yogananda, *Autobiography*, page 154.
3. Wu, page 100.
4. Blyth, *Zen Classics*, II, 33.
5. Ogata, *Transmission* X.20.5.
6. *The Masks of God: Primitive Mythology* (New York: Viking Press, 1959), pages 39-40.
7. Joseph Campbell, *Hero With A Thousand Faces* (New York: Pantheon, 1949), page 28.
8. *Tao Teh Ching*, translated by John C.H. Wu (New York: St. John's University Press, 1961), x, I; xxviii, I; xxviii, 3; lxiv, 6; lxviii; xlix, 2.
9. Merton, xxiii, 7.
10. *Ibid.*
11. Wu, page 37.
12. Wing-Tsit Chan, translator, *The Platform Sutra* (New York: St. John's University Press, 1963), nos. 17-19, 14, 17.
13. *Pi-yen-lu*, case 46; Shaw, page 158.
14. Suzuki, I, 217.

15. Wu, page 203.
16. Reps and Senzaki, page 18.
17. Luk, II, 196.
18. Sigmund Freud, *Wit and Its Relation to the Unconscious*, translated and edited by A.A. Brill, *The Basic Writings of Sigmund Freud* (New York: Modern Library, 1938), page 803.
19. Senzaki and McCandless, page 29.
20. *Zen Buddhism and Psychoanalysis* (New York: Grove Press, 1963), page 87.
21. Merton, xii, I.
22. Friedrich Nietzsche, *Thus Spake Zarathustra*, translated by Thomas Common (New York: Random House, n.d.), pages 23-5.

Epilogue

1. *Vajra Bodhi Sea*, I, 3 (October, 1970), page 40.

Index

Proper names of persons are printed in capitals; books, scriptures, and terms are in italics. In the case of prominent Chinese masters, the Japanese pronunciation is given in parenthesis.

BODHIDHARMA (TA-MO, DARUMA, d. circa 536 CE) 14, 24-5, 28-30, 46, 48, 56, 66, 67, 70, 71, 124, 126
BODHISATTVA 26, 55, 57, 69-74, 79
BUDDHA 16-18, 24, 27, 34, 69-75, 82, 93, 110-111, 129, 132, 155
BUDDHADATTA 154
Buddhata (Buddha-nature) 71, 79, 122, 125, 147
  see also self-nature
buffoonery: of the clown 115
  of Socrates 133
  Zen 35, 38f.
BUNSEI 48
BUSON 83
Butsu Myoko 59-60

CAMPBELL, JOSEPH 160
carnival 41
catharsis (comic) 160-1, 167-8
celebration 34-6, 83, 89-108, 153-7, 158-69
CHANG CHIH-HO 50
CH'ANG-CH'ING (CHOKEI, 854-932) 92, 138
CHANG-HSUAN 78
CHANG SENG-YU 78
CHANG SHENG-WEN 71
CHANG-TSAO 50-51
Cha-no-yu (tea ceremony) 98
CHAO-CHOU (JOSHU, 778-897) 14, 19, 20, 33, 37, 43, 52, 58, 82, 87, 129, 137, 147
CHAO-FANG 78
CHAPLIN, CHARLIE 43, 81
CHEN-CHI 91
CHEN LUNG-HSIN 55
CH'EN-FENG (KEMPO, 9th century) 138
CH'EN-HSIEN 73
CHIANG-TU, Prince 78
CHIA-SHAN (Kozan, d. 881) 86
CHIH-CH'EN (782-865) 90
CHIH-CHANG (CHIJO, 8th century) 136
child 10, 26, 28, 96-7, 108, 158, 160f.
childlikeness 26, 28, 46-7, 158, 160f.
CH'I-LIN (9th century) 57
CH'ING-LUNG 141
Ching Te Ch'uan Teng Lu 40 (see also *Transmission of the Lamp*)
CH'ING-YUAN (SEIGEN, d. 740) 94
CH'IN-NIU (KINGYU, 8th century) 155

184

CH'I-TAN 78
ch'i-yun (vital harmony) 46, 51
choju-giga (animal caricatures) 69
CHOKEI (see CH'ANG-CH'ING)
CHO TAI-SHI (see PU-TAI)
CHOU-FANG 78
CHUANG-TZU (4th century BCE) 62, 77, 115, 119, 122, 134, 162, 168
CHU CHING-HSUAN 49
CHUN, Prince 78
CH'UNG-HUI (d. 779) 91
CHU-TI (GUTEI, d. 9th century) 40, 45, 152, 165
clown: ambiguity of 54, 96, 101, 114
    as religious figure 29, 37-52, 81, 160
    functions of 53-4, 91, 112, 133, 160-1
    invincibility of 120
    suspicion of 17, 28
    symbolism of 29, 42-3, 53-4, 81, 120-1, 160-1
clown-figure: in Zen art 25-9, 41, 44-8, 51-3
    Zen artist as 49-52
    Zen Master as 37-44, 127f.
    frontispiece, plates 1-4, 9-10
coincidentia oppositorum 81
COLLINGWOOD, R.G. 71
comedy: definition 20-1, 33-4, 69, 98, 100, 103
    discussion of 69, 98, 100, 121, 158f.
    levels of 158-69
    low 17-8, 55, 58-9, 61, 129, 137
comic twist 135, 155f.
commonplace: Zen treatment of 23-4, 27-8, 69-108, 164
Confucianism 51, 76
cynicism 101-2

DAISHU (see TAI-CHU)
DAITO 48
dancing 25-6, 30, 46, 101
    plate 3
DARUMA (see BODHIDHARMA)
daruma doll 67
death (in comic perspective) 42, 138-60
DEMARU 27
DESCARTES 111

desire: folly of 113-16
    overcoming 34-5, 48, 120f., 161-2
    vicious circle of 55, 115
despair 101-2
Dhammapada 115
dharma (doctrine, law, way) 17, 24, 66, 74, 82, 128, 131-2, 135, 143-4
    'wordless' 24, 45, 60-6, 82, 127-44, 145-53, 156
Dharmakaya 88, 95
dhyana (meditation) 65, 84-5
dialectical method 138-9
Diamond Sutra (see *Vajracheddika*)
DOGEN (1200-53) 124, 143-4
DORIN (see TAO-LIN)
dragon (as Zen symbol) 22, 24, 27-8, 35, 50
dualism 30, 46, 67-8, 78-81, 85-8, 113-6, 121-2, 131, 161, 167-8

ego: folly of 55, 109-15
    overcoming of 30, 35, 45, 48, 111-15, 117-26, 158-9, 168
EICHO 74
EKA (see HUI-K'O)
EKIDO 164
EMERSON, RALPH WALDO 80
emptiness (see *sunyata*)
ENGO (see YUAN-WU)
enlightenment (see also *satori*) 25, 122-6, 127f., 145f., 153, 158-9
    comic freedom of 48, 62, 95-6, 104, 138, 155, 158f.
    examples of 24, 62, 67, 113-4, 152-3, 159
    'sudden' 123, 127f., 145f.
    test of 31, 36, 114
ENNIN 39
ENO (see HUI-NENG)
EZO (see HUI-TS'ANG)

fall of man (see also Paradise-lost) 117, 160
FA-SHIH 78
FA-YEN (HOGEN, 885-958) 64, 82, 137
FENG SHAO-CHANG 78
Five Lamps Meeting at the Source 142
Finger Pointing at the Moon 142
FO-CHIEN 149
folly 109-126, 127, 129, 151, 154
fool: ambiguity of 54, 96, 101
    as religious figure 29, 37-52, 81, 109, 112, 132-3
    symbolism of 42-3, 45-6, 81, 109, 112, 120-1
    Shakespearean 143

NAGARJUNA 24, 103-4, 130, 139
NAN-CH'UAN (NANSEN, 748-834) 56-7, 62, 65, 94, 127, 147, 149, 158
Nembutsu 59
nenro 64
NIETZSCHE, FRIEDRICH 168-9
Nirvana 27
NIU-T'OU 92, 113
Noh (theatre) 99, 112
non-attachment 113-26
nonsense 20, 30, 35, 45, 101, 121, 135, 140
  of the clown 45
  Zen use of 35, 41, 135, 139-40, 160
NU-YU 162-3

OBAKU (see HUANG-PO)
ordinary mind 87, 94, 164
original mind 94, 124, 131
original nature 123-6, 129, 163-5
  (see also self-nature and *Buddhata*)

PANG CHU-SHIH (HOKOJI, 8th century) 94, 105
P'AN-SHAN (BANZAN) 52
PAO-CH'E (8th century) 38
PAO-FU (HOFUKU, d. 928) 92
PAO-TZU 89
Paradise-lost 160f.
Paradise-regained 160, 167-8
paradox 139
Parinirvana (Supreme Nirvana) 58
PIEN-LUAN 78
Pi-yen-lu (Blue Cliff Records) 150, 156
PLATO 133
play 30, 64, 100, 160
playfulness: levels of 93-4, 138, 160f.
  of children 10, 35, 160-2, 168-9
  of the clown 35, 46-7
  of the master 39-40, 52, 55f., 127f.
  of the *Mondo* 136f.
  of Zen fools 26, 40, 42, 44
  Zen interpretation of 30, 35, 48, 93-4, 136f., 145f., 160f.
p'o-mo (splashed ink) 50-1, 74, 99
PO-CHANG 119, 123
prajna (wisdom, intuitive knowledge) 152
Prajnaparamita Sutra 30, 82, 87

191

PRAJNATARA 76-7
P'U-HUA 159
punctum indifferens 54, 81, 127
puns 96, 136, 140
Pure Land (see also *Jodo Shin-shu*) 72, 78, 83
PU-TAI (HOTEI, d. 916) 25-30, 35, 41, 46-7, 86, 166, 168
  as avatar of MAITREYA 47
  plates 1, 3, 10

RANSETSU 83
RAZAN (see LO-SHAN)
recollection 10, 160-3, 169-70
  Socratic 127-8, 132-4
  Zen 129-32, 133-44, 160f.
Republic 133
RINZAI (see LIN CHI)
Rinzai Sect 41, 123-6
ROWLEY, GEORGE 48-9
RYOKAN (1758-1831) 26, 40, 43

Saddharma-pundarika Sutra 82, 111
sage 10, 25-6, 47, 110-11, 161-3, 166, 168
SAKYAMUNI (GAUTAMA BUDDHA) 59, 70, 73-4, 91
samsara (wheel of rebirth) 55
SAN-SHENG 149
SANTAYANA, GEORGE 69, 103
sanzen (koan session) 123
sarcasm 105
sarira 57, 77
SARTRE, JEAN-PAUL 102
satire 55f., 105
satori (see also enlightenment) 94, 100, 113, 145f.
SEIGEN (see CH'ING-YUAN)
self-nature 120, 123-6, 130, 136, 138, 147, 164
  (see also original nature and *Buddhata)*
SENGAI (1750-1837) 27, 36, 48, 58, 75, 119
  plates 6, 8
senryu 34, 67
SENZAKI, NYOGEN 18
SEPPO (see HSUEH-FENG)
sesshin (week of intensive meditation) 170
SESSHU 71
SETCHO (see HSUEH-T'OU)
SHAKESPEARE 121, 143

195

Lightning Source UK Ltd.
Milton Keynes UK
UKOW06f0736070317

295979UK00001B/213/P